CONTENTS

BURNING SPEAR

Eric Doumerc

With contributions from
Michael Turner
James Danino
David Bousquet
Moqapi Selassie
Roots Knotty Roots

APS Books
Yorkshire

APS Books,
The Stables, Field Lane,
Aberford
West Yorkshire,
LS25 3AE

APS Books is a subsidiary of
the APS Publications imprint

www.andrewsparke.com

Foreword

Winston Rodney, aka Burning Spear, released his latest album, *No Destroyer*, in August 2023, and has been working as a recording artiste since 1969, the year when the epochal "Door Peep" was released. He is considered as a reggae icon and as the "voice" of roots reggae by many reggae fans all over the world.

This book looks at various aspects of Spear's long career, and starts with an annotated discography and biographical chapter which serves an introduction to the next three chapters.

The second chapter examines Burning Spear's work at the legendary Studio One, and was written by David Bousquet, a senior lecturer at the University of Burgundy in France.

The third chapter was penned by the reggae activist and sound system operator James Danino and focuses on Spear's own labels and efforts at self-productions, putting into practice Marcus Garvey's teachings about self-help and independence.

The fourth chapter was written by Moqapi Selassie, a Birmingham-based dub poet and a member of the Rastafarian community who opened for Burning Spear at the Hummingbird, Birmingham, in 2022. Selassie's article provides an insider's perspective on Spear and asks some relevant questions about the relevance and impact of the Rastafarian movement today.

The book closes with a chapter about Spear's legacy and influence.

We hope that this book will be of interest to Spear's fans and reggae fans more generally. Sometimes contrasting perspectives and opinions about Spear will be found in this book. We thought it best to leave them side by side so that the reader can form his or her own opinion. Whether the Spear is still burning bright today is a matter best left to personal judgement.

Eric Doumerc

I
Burning Spear: A Life in Music
(Eric Doumerc)

Winston Rodney was born in 1945 in St Ann's Bay, a fishing port on the North Coast of Jamaica which is the capital of Saint Ann parish. He had a rural upbringing with his eight sisters and four brothers, and this was to have a profound influence on his life and songwriting. His mother was "in the food business" and provided food for people in "construction jobs" (Katz 155), whereas his father "raised chickens" (Katz 155) and was also "in road construction" (Katz 2022). Rodney's parents were Pentecostal Christians and were quite strict: he had to go to church twice a day and "you ain't chickening out on that" (Katz 2022).

The Jamaica where Winston Rodney was born was still a British colony, basically an impoverished former sugar island whose main industry, the sugar trade, had not yet been replaced by tourism and where social inequality and racial stratification were rampant. In 1948 Jamaica was ruled by the Jamaica Labour Party, which had come to power in 1944 after the first elections held under universal suffrage (provided by the new Constitution).

Rodney became interested in music in the late 1950s and early 1960s, and among the musicians he rated highly we find "the great trombone player Don Drummond, the guitarist Ernest Ranglin" (Katz 2022), but also Alton Ellis, The Heptones, Larry Marshall and Peter Tosh: "All those bredren were there before I-man, so I was listening to the real hardcore, I wasn't listening to the fancy side of reggae music. And one of the main people who I was listening to is Bob Marley – I would listen to every one of Bob's songs" (Katz 2022).

After having tried several jobs (he worked as a tiler and as a renovator, but also did some dry cleaning and car washing), Winston Rodney decided to try his hand at song-writing and was advised by a young Bob Marley, also from the parish of Saint Ann, to hook up with Clement "Coxsone" Dodd at Studio One. Rodney met Marley by chance in the heart of Saint Ann's countryside while searching for some marijuana plants: "That area is where most of the herb was cultivated at the time, so we went into that area to get some good smoke. And I saw Bob coming down the street with his donkey and a lot of plants. Bob was going to his farm, doing his own cultivation, and at that time, Rastaman and Rastaman stand firm and was reasoning. I remember asking him how I could get started in this music business and Bob asked I if I know of Studio One" (Katz 2022).

This was in 1969. Jamaica had been independent for seven years, and, as the Barbadian poet and historian Edward Kamau Brathwaite pointed out, the country had entered a period of "post-Independence blues". Indeed Independence had not solved Jamaica's endemic problems and the country was still plagued by rampant poverty, a race-based class system, and a colonial mentality. Dissatisfaction was rife and the "rude-boy phenomenon" between 1965 and 1967 had shown that young people in the working-class areas were becoming restless. The "Rodney Riots", which had followed Walter Rodney's expulsion from the country, had led to violent confrontations between the government and young people.

Apparently, Winston Rodney was also advised to contact Dodd by Lawrence "Jack Ruby" Lindo, an Ocho Rios-based sound-system owner who at the time was looking to go into record production :"There's a place in St.Ann's Bay, we call it Key Largo, where Winston hangs out", says Ruby. "We used to go down there and at one stage, before Winston started recording, I hear him singing the song "Chant Down Babylon" (real title "Door Peep Shall Not Enter"). And I eventually say to him 'bwoy if Downbeat (Clement Dodd) hear them song ya him would record the man, y'know'. And I used to deal with Downbeat, buying dub for my sound system, so I tell him of the artist and he said carry him come make me hear him. Well I tell Spear and he went and deal with Downbeat, and record the song and they start working together" (Gayle, *Black Music*, 32).

Rodney went to Studio One on a Sunday in 1969, accompanied by Rupert Willingston, who had sometimes supported him on harmony when he had sung in St Ann's Bay. The duo were auditioned there by Dodd himself, who liked what he heard : "I came to Studio One and tell Mr Dodd "Bob say   I should come to you", and Mr Dodd say I should sing what I got, and the first song that came out is Door Peeper. And Mr Dodd was happy. He never heard anything like that before, so to him, perhaps this can be gold!" (Katz 2022).Thus "Door Peeper", caught Dodd's fancy and Rodney was told to come back on the Monday to record it. This was the first single Clement Dodd released by a new singer called "Burning Spear". The nom de plume "Burning Spear" is a reference to the Mau Mau leader Jomo Kenyatta, whose nickname was "the burning spear". Rodney was advised to use that nom de plume by a Rastafarian elder called Nyah whom he met in Kingston: "I used to go to Industrial Terrace off Spanish Town Road. That was the joint where you could get your little smoke and drink a beer, talk a little with a guy named GG, a man who love to play him guitar, and there were this man, we call him Nyah" (Katz 2022). Nyah asked Rodney if he had heard of Jomo Kenyatta, the then-current president of Kenya. Nyah told Rodney what the name "Jomo" meant in Kikuyu and told him that it would be a good name "to carry as an artist". Rodney agreed and decided to adopt it as a stage name.

"Door Peeper" was released in 1970 on the Supreme label, and must have sounded rather unusual at the time, as it was closer to a prayer or a hymn than to a pop song. Indeed, the sombre horns and chanting style probably owed more to Rastafarian hymn-singing than to traditional or pop song-writing conventions. In the UK the song appeared on Junior Lincoln's Bamboo label (this label distributed mainly Studio One material) and was distributed through Lincoln's shop.

It must be said that few record producers in Jamaica at the time would have bothered to spend time and money on such uncommercial music. Indeed, when you compare it with the type of Jamaican music that was selling at the time, it is obvious that recording Spear's songs was a "leap of faith", as John Masouri wrote (Masouri, *Reggae Vibes*). Spear's songs were totally different from everything else at the time, and it is very unlikely that Duke Reid or Leslie Long would have even listened to them. Spear remembers that there was a tailor's shop in Saint Ann's Bay where they had recording facilities and where you could cut an acetate record. When he went to that shop with his songs about slavery and Marcus Garvey, he was told that slavery had been abolished a long time ago and that Marcus Garvey had been dead for a long time too. In other words, he was told that no one would bother to listen to these songs.

"Door Peeper" opened with a spectacular horn riff or fanfare played by David Madden and Cedric Brooks who, at the time had replaced Vin Gordon and Glen Da Costa as the main horn section at Studio One. Madden and Brooks were to record several tracks together as "Im and Dave". The song grabs the listener from the first thanks to that great horn riff and never lets go. The songseems to warn against informers and outsiders who spy on Rastafarians and then report what they have seen to the police or the authorities, and it encourages Rastafarians to "chant down Babylon", that is to defeat Babylon with the power of reggae music. The song is introduced by a spoken passage in which Rodney talks about the "sounds of the Burning Spear" and this creates a dramatic effect, as if a roots deejay is addressing his audience directly.

At Studio One, Rodney, or Burning Spear as he was now billed, recorded a number of songs with Rupert Willingston, or sometimes on his own. These songs included "Ethiopians Live It Out", "We Are Free", "Zion Higher", "This Population", "New Civilization", and "He Prayed (aka Joe Frazier")". One of these songs, "He Prayed" was a hit in 1972. It is based on a passage from Matthew's gospel (Matthew 8:20): "The foxes have holes and the birds of the air have nests, but the Son of Man has nowhere to lay His head." The words are sometimes said to imply that Jesus Christ had a hard road to travel and that life was very hard for him, as the early Christians were persecuted by the Romans and had to hide to practice their faith. In an interview granted to David Katz, Spear stressed the universal meaning of the song: "In the song, I speak about Jah prayed for I and you, until his sweat turned [to] blood. I don't deal with colourism, nationality, or religion; I say glory be to Jah, the creator. We give thanks to the universe, to nature" (Katz 2022). Another outstanding Studio One single released in 1972 was "New

Civilization" on which Spear sang with an uncredited Larry Marshall and was accompanied by Roy Richard on harmonica (Michael Turner, 2004).

In 1973 Clement Dodd released Burning Spear's first album, entitled *Studio One Presents Burning Spear*, which included many songs Rodney was to redo later on his Island albums: "Ethiopians Live It Out", "Fire Down Below", "Creation Rebel", "Door Peep Shall Not Enter", and "Down By The Riverside". The other tracks on the album were "We Are Free", "Don't Mess With Jill", "Pick Up The Pieces", "Ready", "Journey", "Them a Come", and "He Prayed".

The album first came out in a white sleeve when first imported into the UK by Daddy Peckings, and was released with a different cover a few months later (Chris Lane, email communication).

Several of these early songs by Burning Spear addressed the theme of the resilience of black people in the face of slavery and their ability to survive. For instance, "Ethiopians Live It Out" listed the various ethnic groups who had come to or been forcefully imported into Jamaica over the course of its troubled history and came to the conclusion that out of the Chinese, the Syrians, the Africans, and the Indians, only the "Ethiopians" had managed to "live it out", that is to survive the experience of chattel slavery. The song is notable for its use of the call and response pattern, a feature to be found in numerous black musical forms, and in its use of the word "Ethiopians" to refer to the Africans who were sold into slavery. This word has of course Biblical connotations as there are many passages in the Bible referring to Ethiopia. Moreover the word "Ethiopia" seems to have been used by the ancient Greeks to refer to the African continent. "Ethiopians Live It Out" met with success in 1974 and Rodney considers it his first real hit (Forgie, *Jamaica Daily News*).

The song entitled "Fire Down Below" seems to take as its main theme the explosive situation at the time (the early 1970s) through the metaphor of tea drinking. In a 1976 *Race and Class* article, Linton Kwesi Johnson analysed the lyrics of that song in detail and concluded that the teapot represents the collective experience of the people, the cup of tea is the nourishment they derive from that experience, and the hot and scalding tea symbolises the danger that if you do not tip the pot over, it will overflow and will burn you. Johnson teases out some of the most profound meanings in that song and shows us that when his article was published (in 1976) Burning Spear's lyrics had already made an impact in the UK among the Black British and Jamaican expatriate population: "The historical experience of the Afro-Jamaican is here likened unto a journey through history, the sea of time, on the ship of life. But as the ship of life sails on the sea of history, all is not well aboard. There is "fire/down below": there is repression, rebellion, poverty, and despair. And the people are disorganized, and disunited, and "the people dem a running around/and the people dem a running around". Then Johnson explains that the people who are struggling will be strengthened by their "cup of tea" which represents "spiritual nourishment". They then will know how to derive strength from their collective experience and will eventually rebel, but in a sober way, and they will "tip it over" so that their passion will be controlled and will not scald them. In his article, Johnson calls Spear a "political culturalist" and makes it clear that Spear's songs had by then a had a significant impact on the Caribbean and Black British community in Britain.

1974 saw the release of a second album on Studio One entitled *Rocking Time*, which contained tunes like "Foggy Road", "Swell Headed", "Call On You", "Bad to Worst", "Call On You", "Walla Walla", "Rocking Time", Weeping and Wailing", "Mamie", "Old Time Saying", "What a Happy Day", "Girls Like You", and "This Race".

"Foggy Road" is a hypnotic chant which works as a metaphor both for Spear's own situation then and for the plight of black people. Indeed he sang that his way was long and that the road was foggy, but that Jah was his "eyesight" and would help him defeat his enemies.

"Swell Headed" is a proud declaration of independence as he states that he will never run away but remains humble in the face of adversity.

"This Race" is based on Ecclesiastes 9:11 ("The race is not to the swift, Nor the battle to the strong, Nor bread to the wise, Nor riches to men of understanding, Nor favor to men of skill; But time and chance happen to them all"), but Spear adapted the biblical text to suit his purpose: "This race is not for the swift, but for the smart".

The musicians who played on these Studio One tracks included, at various stages, Leroy Sibbles, who was there when Spear first auditioned for Dodd and who played bass on Spear's first album , the drummer Leroy "Horsemouth" Wallace, and The Gladiators, who were Studio One's backing band for a number of years. Apparently Leroy Sibbles played a major part in auditioning Rodney and helped him develop musically: "When we heard them, it was like a joke.... It was a new sound, Rasta men coming in from the country. A lot of people weren't interested; but I liked it, and I worked on the first album they did. I produced it, and I played on it; I got them started," (Howell, Peter."Jamaica Beckons and Sibbles is Listening."*Toronto Star* 26 April 1991, quoted by Lauren Maccuaig). Other musicians who backed Spear up on some songs included David Madden and Cedric Brooks (for instance on "Door Peeper"), Ernest Ranglin, Fil Callender, Pablove Black, and Jackie Mittoo. The Soul Defenders, who were the Studio One backing band in the early 1970s, also worked with Spear on some songs. This band included Joseph Hill, who was to find fame as the lead singer with Culture later on, and he sang harmony.

The great Larry Marshall, who was a recording artist in his own right, but also worked at Studio One as an arranger, worked with Rodney on quite a few of his songs:"I first met Spear when I went to St Ann's Bay with Jackie Mittoo, for a show in Sommerville. I went around to the beach to find a smoke. Because I smoked then. And I see a lot of smoke, and Burning Spear came up to me, and say "Mr Marshall, I would like to do some recording, but don't know how to go about it". So, I said "Find your way to Studio One and I'll set you up. Then he goes to Jack Ruby, and there he rehearses and rehearses with this band.

And he bring them to record with Coxsone- the Soul Defenders. I was the one to help him, show him how to sing and portray this African sound. All those [Burning Spear] songs I know because I helped arrange them."(Barrow and Dalton 95).

Burning Spear's work at Studio One between 1969 and 1974 made quite an impact with other Studio One artists and it is obvious that he was an inspiration for a few of them. Whether we are talking about instrumentals, dub tracks or simply new songs on Spear's "riddims", Winston Rodney's music clearly resonated with many Studio One artistes.

"Door Peep Shall Not Enter" (aka "Door Peeper"), Spear's first song recorded at Studio One, gave rise to Prince Jazzbo's "Imperial I", a song of praise addressed to Jah Rastafari which is also a call for African unity.

"We Are Free" inspired Jackie Mittoo to record "Wild Bunch", maybe named after the famous western of the same name.

"Creation Rebel" gave birth to "Creation Skank" by Prince Jazzbo, a toast in the vein of what Big Youth was doing at the time. Jazzbo rhymes "rebel" with "devil" ("debil") and riffs on the theme of being a rebel. Jazzbo borrows from current deejay patter as pioneered by U-Roy and Big Youth. Other versions inspired by "Creation Rebel included "Creation" by Dub Specialist, "Ready Natty Dready" by Dillinger, and "Without You" by the Wailing Souls.

Dillinger's "Ready Natty Dreadie" riffs on the Natty Dread theme, as Big Youth and Bob Marley had done before him. Dillinger's track was on his seminal eponymous album (1975).

The Wailing Souls' "Without You" is a beautiful love song about a man who cannot live without his lover, with a great vocal by Winston McDonald.

"Don't Mess With Jill" inspired Dub Specialist's "Brial Wisp", named after a Jamaican plant. The track was featured on the *Roots Dub* LP, together with the "Saucy Perila" track.

"Pick Up The Pieces" led to Dub Specialist's "Roaring Reggae" and also inspired Im and David's "Soul Walk"

"Get Ready" spawned a dub by the Brentford Rockers, as well as

"Jah Jah Help Us" by Big Joe, and "Love Jah Jah" by Winston Jarrett.

"He Prayed" moved Dennis Alcapone to record "Joe Frazier Round 2", a tribute to the American boxer who had won the heavy-weight world championship the year before, in 1973.

"Happy Valley" by the little-known Rheuben Alexander is a horn workout over Spear's heavy backing track and eventually merges into jazz. "He Prayed" also inspired the Righteous Flames, Winston Jarrett's group, to come up with "Solid Foundation". Jarrett's track works well with Spear's lyrics and sounds as if it was recorded at the same time, a bit like a deejay track.

"Call On You" gave birth to "Everyday Skank" (Im and David) and "Scatter Rock" (Brentford Disco Set).

"Foggy Road" gave rise to a deejay-style track by the Jay Tees who told their audience about "Buck Town Corner" and displayed their deejay skills over Spear's rocking riddim while Pablove Black celebrated "High Locks" with his melodica, showing he had listened well to Augustus Pablo. Pablove Black was further inspired to record versions of "Swell Headed" ("Dread Head" and "Push Pull").

The beautiful and heartfelt "What A Happy Day" encouraged Delroy Wilson to "Keep on Trying".

"This Race" was followed by a dub by Dub Specialist and inspired the song "Stick Together" by the Classics (Wailing Souls)

"Rocking Time" led to "Fear Not" by Winston Jarrett, while Prince Jazzbo came up with "Pepper Rock", a version which shows how influential Dennis Alcapone was at the time. Jazbbo even quoted a few lines from "Mosquito One". "Rocking Time" also gave birth to the dub track "Saucy Perila" by Dub Specialist.

"Zion Higher" (on the album *Jamaican All-Stars Vol.2*) gave birth to "Nite Ride" by Im and David whereas "This Population" (on *Pirates Choice*) inspired Jackie Mittoo to record "Happy People" (the track was featured on his *Macka Fat* album).

"Swell Headed" was another hit in 1975, but Spear felt that his first producer, Clement Dodd, had not rewarded him sufficiently, and due to financial disagreements, he left Studio One. Spear decided to take a break from the music business and to move back to Saint Ann's Bay to think about his next move. By then he had become disillusioned with the way Coxsone had treated him and went back to his old job (he was a tiler and a renovator by trade). Then he was struck by the fact that he lived in Saint Ann's Bay, which was also the birthplace of Marcus Garvey, and that he had not heard a singer sing about Garvey yet. He began to think about how modern slavery still existed and came to the conclusion that things had not changed much. That was how the songs "Marcus Garvey" and "Slavery Days" came to him.

With "Marcus Garvey", and "Slavery Days" under his belt, Spear tried to negotiate a deal with Laurence "Jack Ruby" Lindo, an Ocho Rios-based sound system entrepreneur who wanted to go into music production. But this time he took care to ask for some advance money first. No more would he be stung by record producers.

Lawrence Lindo was a sound system proprietor based in Ocho Rios who had wanted to go into the music business for a long time when he met Rodney. He was well connected and knew Clement Dodd, who had supplied him with dub plates in the past. Lindo had been mischievously nicknamed "Jack Ruby" by his colleagues when he was working in a hotel on the north coast of Jamaica in the 1960s because he had been calling everyone "Jackson". Lindo had been championing Spear's music for quite a few years on his sound system, and was looking to go into record production. So Spear's departure from Studio One came in the nick of time for his career. Jack Ruby insisted on Spear using two backing vocalists and Rupert Willingston was once again recruited, together with another St Ann's Bay singer, Delroy Hines (Justin Hines's brother).

Ruby approached Spear as he had heard that he had two new songs, and they eventually recorded a song entitled "Marcus Garvey" in late 1974 for sound system use only. The song became so popular that Ruby had to release it as a 45 on his Fox label.

By 1975, "Marcus Garvey" and Spear's Studio One material had made him a star in Jamaica and in May 1975 he performed at the Carib Theatre in Kingston as part of the Easter Magic show. On that day Rodney was assisted by Delroy Hines and Rupert Willingston on harmony, and they were backed by the Third World Band. In his May 1975 article for the *Jamaica Daily News,* Andell Forgie wrote that Spear "brought the house down" when he performed "Foggy Road" as an encore, leaving the audience screaming for more.

Then "Slavery Days" came out as a 45 and confirmed Spear's popularity. Ruby then took Spear to Randy's studio for the recording of the *Marcus Garvey* album. The Fox 45s had sold very well and had prepared Spear's fans for the album that was to come.

The *Marcus Garvey* album was recorded at Randy's studio and featured such stellar musicians as Robbie Shakespeare, Leroy "Horsemouth" Wallace, Earl "Chinna" Smith, Tyrone Downie, Bernard "Touter" Harvey, and the famous Burning Spear horns, Bobby Ellis on trumpet, Vincent Gordon on trombone, and Richard "Dirty Harry" Hall on saxophone. These horns were to play a fundamental part in the career of Burning Spear. These musicians became collectively known as the Black Disciples.

The *Marcus Garvey* album is often credited with launching the new fashion for songs about or in praise of Marcus Garvey, but, surprisingly, the album contains only two songs about the Saint Ann prophet. But these two songs were strategically situated at the beginning of the two sides of the original LP. The two songs, "Marcus Garvey" and "Old Marcus Garvey", set the scene for each side, so to speak, and serve as introductions to the themes developed in the other songs.

The song "Marcus Garvey" opens the first side and is a retelling of a story which had been part of the Jamaican oral tradition for a very long time and which presented Garvey as a Christ-like figure who had been betrayed by one of his associates, one Bag-O-Wire. According to Barry Chevannes, Bag-O-Wire was a semi-legendary mad derelict (Chevannes 107) who had betrayed Marcus Garvey for a plate of rice and peas, just like Judas who had betrayed Jesus for a mess of pottage, and as a result he had been cursed. His curse was that he was to roam the streets of Kingston forever. His nickname came from the fact that he was dressed in a burlap bag which was pratically threadbare, with the metal bits showing, hence his nickname "bag-o-wire" (Chevannes 107).

Spear's song gave rise to an equally forceful and popular "version" by the charismatic deejay Big Youth (Manley Buchanan), who by then was probably the most popular deejay in Jamaica. Big Youth's version, entitled "Mosiah Garvey", extended Spear's message and enhanced it by adding his own prophecies like "Bag-O-Wire ketch a fire!" and "The righteous black man shall stand while the weakheart black man shall fall !". Youth's fiery delivery was full of dread and indignation as he detailed Garvey's prophetic message: as he passed through the door of Spanish Town prison, no other prisoner would go through this door. Big Youth also reminded his audience that Garvey had prophesied that black people would never know themselves until their backs were against the wall. At times Big Youth sounds like a charismatic preacher on this track. Big Youth begins by reminding people that "certain places in King Street" are now a car park, thus alluding to the fact that the place where the headquarters of Garvey's Universal Negro Improvement Association were situated (on King Street) had been turned into a car park. So right from the start Big Youth insists that Garvey is an unsung hero of the black cause and that his memory must be kept alive.

The second paean to Garvey, "Old Marcus Garvey", opens the second side and bemoans the fact that "no one remembers" Garvey and that other famous Jamaican leaders like Paul Bogle, William Gordon, George Washington Manley, and Alexander Bustamante had been made "National Heroes" whereas Garvey had not been granted this honour. In that song, Garvey is likened to John The Baptist, who was beheaded and to the martyr Stephen, who was stoned to death. So Garvey iks presented as a martyr for the black cause and a Christ-like figure.

So the two Garvey-themed songs present Marcus Garvey as an important prophet who was betrayed and rejected by his own people who do not remember him today. He is a presented as an important semi-biblical character cast in the same mould as John

The Baptist who baptised Jesus Christ and ended up being beheaded, and Saint Stephen, an early martyr who was stoned to death. This mythological view of Garvey sets the stage for Spear's journey into the Jamaican oral tradition and into black history which occupies most of the album.

After "Marcus Garvey", the first side continues with "Slavery Days", with its insistent refrain and call and response structure, actually reminiscent of a work-song. The song addresses the delicate issue of slavery and in 1975 Jamaica, caused quite a stir, prompting Jamaicans to take a look at their own history. The song is an important moment in Jamaica's post-colonial history and its impact cannot be overestimated.

After "Slavery Days" came, in a very logical way, "The Invasion", which condems in no uncertain terms the cultural ravages perpetrated by colonialism on Caribbean people, but which nevertheless insists on the theme of love through its chorus ("Wadada" means "Love" in Amharic). The sombre bass line and haunting refrain make that song particularly effective. Jackie Edwards covered the track in 1976.

Side one concludes with two more soothing tracks, "Live Good" and "Give Me", which look at the need to build a new culture after the trauma of slavery and address the themes of cultural reconstruction and regeneration.

After "Old Marcus Garvey", the second side continues with "Tradition", a track which was apparently inspired by a tradItional song from Saint Ann and establishes a link between the slave trade, slavery, and African retentions in the Caribbean. It makes its point very simply through the call and response pattern. In an interview granted to Vivien Goldman, Spear revealed an unexpected side of his personality when he expatiated on the genesis of "Tradition". He explained that in the days of slavery the slaves were not allowed to communicate when they passed one another and that they simply kept their heads down in order to avoid punishment. So they kept on "trodding" and indulged in "tradition" ("troddition"). Spear was here delving into the Rastafarian tradition of reasoning, which often leads to lingusitic manipulations and punning.

"Jordon River" is probably a Jamaican take on the African-American spiritual "Roll, Jordan, Roll" which identifies the Jordan River as a symbol of freedom and hope. Indeed in the 19th century African-Americans reintepreted Methodist or Baptist hymns to tell their own story and "Roll Jordan, Roll" is a version of an earlier hymn by the English Methodist preacher Charles Wesley. The slaves reinterpreted Wesley's message of hope and the Jordan River in his hymn came to refer to the Ohio River, or to the Mississippi. In the Bible, the Jordan River is mentioned in connection with the Israelites' flight from Egypt and with their arrival in the Promised Land. It seems to symbolise the last obstacle to be overcome before freedom can be tasted. The Jordan River is also the place where John the Baptist baptised Jesus Christ.

"Red Gold and Green" is the only Rastafarian or Rasta-inspired song on the album, thus contrasting sharply with "Jordon River" and its Christian imagery. In "Red Gold and Green" we hear about a different type of Promised Land where the lion "crowned the king" in Addis-Ababa, an obvious reference to the coronation of Haile Selassie in Ethiopia and to Ethiopia's status as the rastas' Promised Land.

The album closes with "Resting Place" which delves into the Bible once again with the idea of the "resting place", which seems to echo the theme developed in "He Prayed".

The impact of Burning Spear's first album cannot be overestimated. It took Jamaica by storm and made a very big impression on a new generation of singers like Joseph Hill and The Mighty Diamonds. Several songs on the album were covered by other reggae artists: Third World recorded "Slavery Days" for their first album, Joe Higgs recorded a sequel entitled "More Slavery", Jackie Edwards cut his own version of "The Invasion", Johnny Clarke recorded "Ites, Green and Gold", and the Cimarons offered their own rendition of "Tradition". So all of a sudden Burning Spear was the new reggae sensation and the *Marcus Garvey* album received favourable reviews, although his dub companion, *Garvey's Ghost*, was not so well received, presumably on account of the mix that Island Records proposed.

Marcus Garvey was followed by *Man In The Hills,* which also featured the harmonies of Rupert Willlingston and Delroy Hines. The album was recorded at Harry J's and Randy's studios and was characterised by a brighter sound than its predecessor. Contrary to the *Marcus Garvey* album, it seems to be based on childhood reminiscences associated with the rural lifestyle Spear experienced in Saint Ann's Bay.

The title track powerfully evokes the daily tasks or chores that people living in the hills have to carry out: going to the river to get some water, gathering "bramble" to start a fire, washing the dishes, going to the local grocer's shop to get some food. Spear mentions his father working in the fields. Rodney's mother provided meals for construction workers and his father raised chickens. The song is based on a simple, hypnotic chorus ("And if we should live up in the hills"). The hills in Jamaica are often associated with a new life away from the plantations after the abolition of slavery and with the appearance of "Free Villages" which were founded with the help of the Non-Conformist chapels like the Baptists and the Methodists. The man in the hills referred to in the song could have been a peasant cultivator or an independent farmer eking out a living on a small plot of land in the hills after slavery.

The second track, entitled 'It Is Good", can be considered as a declaration of independence on Spear's part and makes the simple point that "it is good when a man can think for himself", repeated over and over again. A sturdy independence of mind is advocated here as the antidote to the poison of colonisation and oppression. But the song can also be interpreted as a call for unity in the context of the 1976 elections in Jamaica which pitted the PNP against the JLP and resulted in a very high number of deaths. The reference to the games played by politicians ("tribal war" and "hide and seek") could be interpreted in that light, or in the broader context of human relationships.

That said, the song could be evidence of Garvey's influence as the Saint Ann prophet is supposed to have said: "We want our people to think for themselves" (*Abeng*'s masthead, 1969). Garvey's insistence on the necessity to think for oneself also ties in with his encouragement to "emancipate oneself from mental slavery".

"Black Soul" traces Spear's roots back to Africa and features a long, emotional and heart-felt tribute to his ancestors.

"No More war" seems to bemoan the political violence which had engulfed Jamaica by the mid-1970s with the politicisation of ghettoes and the widespread use of firearms by both political parties. The word "war" is used here to refer to political violence, as in Max Romeo's "War In Babylon", which was also released in 1976.

The song entitled "Children" is a wonderful cautionary tale, warning children about the dangers awaiting them if they venture near the ocean and asking them to be careful ("Leave the ocean and come"). When the current is too strong and the sea is rough, all kinds of dangers can prey upon little children.

"People Get Ready" is not a cover of the Curtis Mayfield song and uses some train imagery to insist on the need for black unity. Like "No More War", it calls for an end to the tribal war which was tearing Jamaica apart in 1976.

This album also features a new version of "Door Peeper Shall Not Enter", Spear's first tune which was recorded at Studio One in 1969, as well as two tunes which seem to have been recorded with a different audience in mind, "Lion" and "Groovy". These songs seem to have been targeted at the dancehalls and are based on highly danceable rhythms.

Man In The Hills was followed by two albums released in 1977: *Dry And Heavy* and *Live!*, which was recorded at the Rainbow Theatre in October 1977.

Dry and Heavy marked the end of Spear's collaboration with Jack Ruby, and all his subsequent albums were self-produced. Spear wanted to be artistically independent, but his separation with Ruby was amicable and he still has respect for him: "Jack was a good producer because Jack was a music lover. If Jack sees something in any young person out there, Jack would try to help them, musically" (Katz 2022).

By 1977 Burning Spear was no longer a harmony trio as Rodney had decided to part company with Rupert Willingston and Delroy

Hines. In an interview granted to Vivien Goldman and which eventually appeared in the *New Musical Express*, Spear was quite candid about the reason why he had to let these two harmony singers go: they were not dedicated enough to the music and he felt that he literally had to "beg" them to come to the recording studio for rehearsals, and even then they would do so grudgingly.

The musicians who played on the *Dry and Heavy* album were still the Black Disciples, that is Leroy "Horsemouth" Wallace on drums, Bernad "Touter" Harvey and Earl "Wya" Lindo on keyboards, Aston Barrett and Robbie Shakespeare on drums, Scully Simms on percussion, and the great horn section composed of Bobby Ellis, Herman Marquis, Vincent Gordon, and Richard "Dirty Harry" Hall. That horn sections was responsible for crafting the hypnotic and mesmerising Burning Spear sound, with Bobby Ellis as the main arranger. An important contribution to that album was made by Donal Kinsey (mentioned as "Roots Kinsey" in the credits), the American blues guitarist who played with The Wailers on Bob Marley's *Rastaman Vibration* album. Kinsey's blues stylings really enhanced the musical backing on *Dry and Heavy* and complemented Spear's voice nicely.

Dry and Heavy opens with "Any River", a reworking of the Studio One song "Down By The Riverside", a composition that works both as a love song and as a cultural statement. On first listen, it is a paean to the love of Spear's life, but Spear makes the point that this woman could be from Africa, from America, or from Jamaica, meaning she could be any black woman. Likewise, the river mentioned in the song could be "Dunn's River or Key Largo ", the beach in Saint Ann's Bay where Spear used to hang out with Jack Ruby, but it could be any river in the world.

In fact on this album Spear reworked several old songs that he had recorded at Studio One in the early 1970s: "The Sun" is in fact "Calling", "Its' a Long Way Round" is a new version of "Creation Rebel", "I.WI.N." is a reworking of "This Race", and "Black Disciples" is a new cut of "Swell-Headed", which was a hit in 1974. The new versions are of course very well produced and the horns play a very important part in the impact they make on listeners.

The title track ("Dry and Heavy") continues the theme of rural life developed in *Man In The Hills* and takes us back to Spear's school days when he had to carry wood for his family.

"Wailing" is based on the biblical warning that "there shall be weeping, wailing, and gnashing of teeth" and also on a passage from James's Gospel ("to him who knows to do good and does not do *it,* to him it is sin", James 4:17) , while "Shout It Out" ends the album on a very positive note, with Rodney's shout ("Freedom !") echoing in a spectacular fade-out.

By then Spear had already established a solid body of work and had become a cultural hero in Jamaica and in Great Britain where, according to David Hinds, his popularity led to the development of the Rastafarian movement there. Spear's popularity in the UK led to a concert at the Rainbow Theatre in October 1977. In fact Spear turned up in London with no backing band, and a band had to be quickly found to back him up on stage. That band turned out to be Aswad, the young lions of British reggae. They rehearsed relentlessly for three days and eventually did a very good job of backing Spear. Spear's percussionist Philip Fullwood and his trumpet player Bobby Ellis were also part of the band that backed Spear on that seminal show. The late Ghanian saxophonist George Lee was there too. Courtney Hemmings was on keyboards and Brinsley Forde on rhythm guitar. Donald Griffiths was on lead guitar.

Spear's set on that night included three songs from the *Marcus Garvey* album ("Marcus Garvey", "Slavery Days", and "Old Marcus Garvey"), three tracks from the *Man In The Hills* LP ("Lion", the title track, and "Black Soul") and one song from *Dry and Heavy* ("Throw Down Yours Arms"). The album has its moments, with a spectacular rendition of "Man In The Hills" complete with birdcall and jungle noises courtesy of Spear himself and a moving interpretation of "Slavery Days" with Spear asking "Do you ? Do you?", as if he was asking members of the audience about their personal reminiscences about slavery. "Black Soul" obviously resonated with the audience too. Spear went on a long, improvisatory riff on "Black Soul", as he did on several other songs that night. The album was proof that Spear could indeed hypnotise a crowd, as he had done in 1974 in Toronto and in the same year in Jamaica at the Carib Theatre. By the time the *Live!* Album came out, his reputation as an entrancing performer was well established.

The *Live!* album was also an important milestone for the growth of "British reggae" as, at the time, few people believed that classic or "real" reggae could be produced in England. This is what Brisnley Forde, Aswad's vocalist and rhythm guitarist, explained to David Katz: "It was one of the first times that people really began to break down the stigma that classic reggae music couldn't be made in England, 'cos there we were, a British band, playing with Burning Spear (Katz 2002).

Spear's next effort was the album entitled *Marcus' Children*, which was originally released in Jamaica on Spear's label but had a very short shelf life and was eventually rereleased by Island on its subsidiary, One Stop, with a new title, *Social Living*. The new title was a reference to the song of the same name whose refrain was: "Don't you know social living is the best ?", a plea for peace and unity. The album came out in 1978 and was recorded with members of Aswad (Angus Gaye, Brinsley Forde, George Oban, and Courtney Hemmings), the band who had backed Spear on his London concerts in 1977. The album was very much built around the mythical figure of Garvey, with four tracks ("Marcus Children Suffer", "Marcus Say Jah No Dead", "Marcus Senior", and "Mister Garvey") directly referencing the Saint Ann prophet. The album also featured a recut of Spear's Studio One song "He Prayed", retitled "Institution" here (which was also released as a twelve-inch). "Nyath Keith" was a new version of "Zion Higher", also recorded at Studio One in the early 1970s.

In 1994 the Blood and Fire label reissued this album, with liner notes by Steve Barrow, who identified the album as the climax or the summation of what Spear had been trying to do since the early 1970s, that is synthesizing aspects of Garveyism and Rastafarianism to sing about black oppression, black pride, and black culture. According to Barrow, the album was a convincing synthesis of the previous albums Spear had released on Island.

The 1994 reissue gave rise to some very positive reviews, like the one which appeared in the American music magazine *The Beat*. Indeed in his review Richard Henderson likened the album to Marvin Gaye's *What's Going On* album on account of its forward-thinking approach and genre-busting qualities. Henderson compared Spear's approach to the Japanese director Yasujiro Ozu's simple but effective approach, based on simple, traditional values associated with the past. Henderson also pointed out the influence of Black American popular music, notably wah-wah guitars and keyboards. Henderson considered Spear's album as the equivalent of Gaye's landmark opus on account of its thematic unity which made it very much like a concept album.

Two tracks in particular, "Marcus Senior" and "Mister Garvey" turn Garvey into a mythical figure roaming the Jamaican countryside, "from parish to parish", "from district to district", relentlessly spreading the new gospel of black pride. On "Mister Garvey", a trance-like effect is achieved through a riff on the words "cool", "smooth" and "school" which are endlessly repeated and mesh with the horns in the background. "Marcus Say Jah No Dead" is Spear's answer to those who claimed that Haile Selassie's death in 1975 meant the end of Rastafari. Bob Marley had released "Jah Live" to voice many Rastas' feelings about this event, and the singer Junior Byles had suffered a nervous breakdown as a consequence. So Selassie's passing had a massive impact in the Rastafarian community and many Rastas interpreted the reporting of his death as an attack on or a questioning of the Rastas' faith.

The album was the last album Spear recorded with The Black Disciples, the group of musicians who had played on the *Marcus Garvey, Man In The Hills*, and *Dry and Heavy* albums.

Along with the Island releases, Spear was at the time maintaining an activity as an independent producer and had started the Spear label on which he had begun to release his own productions, like "Travelling" (a version of the Studio One tune "Journey"), "Institution", "Spear Burning", and "Jah No Dead". He also released songs by his friend Philip Fullwood ("Thanks and Praise", "I Gave You My Word") and by the artist Burning Junior ("On That Day"). "Travelling" was to become popular with the

London-based producer and sound system operator Lloyd Coxsone who released a dub version of that tune on his *King of the Dub Rock* album.

1978 was also the year when Spear was given a cameo appearance in the film *Rockers*. In a key scene in that film, Spear can be seen singing "Marcus Say Jah No Dead" song a cappella while he sits on the bank of a river with his friend Leroy "Horsemouth" Wallace, who is badly in need of comfort. It is a moving and powerful rendering of that song, with only the sound of tree frogs as accompaniment.

In 1979 Spear's career was given another boost when he performed as part of the Reggae Sunsplash festival held in Montego Bay along with Bob Marley and other artists. He sang "Foggy Road", "Slavery Days", and "Calling" and was interviewed by a team of German journalists who were making a film about Jamaican music at the time. The film would later be released as *Reggae Sunspslash 1979*. In the interview, Spear insisted on the values of togetherness ("Everything we do together!") and unity that he was trying to convey and to him that took the form of the Marcus Garvey Spiritual Centre that he had founded near Key Largo Beach in Saint Ann's Bay. The interview portrays Spear as an eager and driven young Rasta on a mission but also enjoying his favourite pastime, football.

Spear started the new decade with a powerful masterpiece, *Hail H.I.M*, released in 1980 on the EMI label. The album was co-produced by Aston "Family Man" Barrett and was recorded at Tuff Gong Studios. It contains mainly cultural tracks and is probably one of Spear's most "militant" albums, with the opening track, "Columbus", addressing the themes of the colonisation of the Caribbean and the rewriting of History by the colonial authorities. Spear calls Columbus "a damn-blasted liar" and reminds us that the Arawaks were there "before him". As he says, it is a "whole heap of a mix-up, mix-up". Despite its militant outlook, the song has a bright sound with jaunty horns and a bouncing rhythm which contrast with the dark and sombre approach to be found on the *Marcus Garvey* album. Spear's sentiments on that song with his characterisation of Columbus as a liar echo Peter Tosh's "You Can't Blame The Youth" as well as the Calypsonian Shadow's track entitled "Columbus Lied".

The album also includes a new version of "Foggy Road", retitled "Road Foggy" here, as well as two outstanding cultural statements, "African Teacher" and "African Postman", about the necessity to learn Amharic and various aspects of African culture and the necessity to relocate to Africa. The African postman brings a telegram which urges all exiled Africans to relocate to Africa, a powerful metaphor indeed. "Cry Blood Africa" and "Jah A Go Raid" address the themes of the atrocities committed in Africa and the Caribbean in the name of civilisation. Aston Barrett's percussive and dynamic bass lines really contribute a lot to this album and to its highly rhythmic quality. For instance, Barrett's bassline on "African Postman" is played the way a drum would be played.

The 1980s were a troubled period for Jamaican music, with the death of Bob Marley, its greatest spokesperson, the rise of the dancehall movement, and the violent deaths of the dub poet Michael Smith, Hugh Mundell, and the deejay Prince Far-I.

Burning Spear did not release any album in 1981, but 1982 saw the release of *Farover* on the American Heartbeat label. This launched Spear's collaboration with Heartbeat, an American label based in Cambridge, Massachusetts, which was to play a major part in the marketing and promotion of Spear's music in the United States and all over the world. The Heartbeat albums were indeed very well distributed and commercialised in Europe too. The back cover featured a great shot of Spear's Burning Band on a hill overlooking Kingston. Like *Hail H.I.M*, the album was recorded at Tuff Gong Studio and is a Burning Spear production. It is the first Burning Spear album to have been distributed by an American label and is thus proof that Burning Spear's music was beginning to make an impact beyond Jamaica and Britain, with the USA as the next step in his growing global reach.

The album contains two re-cuts of Studio One classics ("She's Mine" is in fact "Don't Mess With Jill" and 'Rock" is a new version of "Rocking Time"). The two standout tracks seem to be "Image" (on the A side on the original LP) and "O' Jah" (on the B side) which are trance-laden and hypnotic paeans to Marcus Garvey and Jah Rastafari respectively.

The album closes with "Jah Is My Driver", a statement of faith which neatly explains Spear's commitment to Rastafari. In an interview published in *The Beat* in 1989, Spear explained what he had tried to do with that song: "Well, the concept of "Jah Is My Driver" is a level of guidance with protection, and knowing that all these motor vehicles built by man, and no time you know when something will be going wrong. So at all time you have to remember Jah. Knowing that when you start the engine, is Jah who start it for you, regardless is your hand holding the key and turning it, and when you press the accelerator, is Jah who is pressing it, for is Jah who give it that life and that energy, and that understanding to know how to do these things. So Jah is the driver !" (Ed Paladino, *The Beat*, April 1989).

In "Greetings" Spear was reaching out to his black brothers in America and lamenting the fact that they did not seem to be interested in finding out more about their history and culture.

1983 saw Spear perform at the Reggae Sunsplash festival and give a moving rendition of "Slavery Days" . He also released an album entitled *The Fittest of the Fittest* on the EMI label. The album was recorded at Tuff Gong Studio and features some stellar musicianship by the Burning Band.

It is a scintillating album, with very warm tones and a bright mix. Spear's militancy is well to the front on tunes like "Repatriation" and the title track. The original LP was divided into a "militant" A side and a softer, warmer B side. The A side included the title track, "Repatriation" and "Old Boy Garvey" as well as a new version of two Studio One songs ("Bad to Worst" and "Fire Man"). Spear thus continued the tradition of revisiting his Studio One legacy.

The B side included more meditative and contemplative songs like "In Africa" and "Vision", as well as a love song ("For You") which is another Studio One recut ("Girls Like You"). "In Africa" is in fact a new version of the Studion One hit "Ethiopians Live It Out" whereas "Vision" is an Pan-Africanist paean which envisions Africa and Jamaica as "one big family".

By then Burning Spear had become the voice of conscious, Rasta-inspired reggae and had built a solid body of work based on the personality of Marcus Garvey, and the themes of repatriation and black liberation. As Steve Barrow wrote in the liner notes to the 1994 Blood and Fire release of *Social Living*, Spear's music made many people aware of the importance of Marcus Garvey and, as Barrow insisted, many people had probably never heard of Garvey before listening to Spear's records. So, in that sense, David Hinds is probably correct when he insists that Burning Spear was responsible for popularizing Rastafarianism in the UK. Spear's music has a strong didactic quality and he made it his mission to teach the whole world about the importance of Garveyism.

By the time *The Fittest of the Fittest* was released, Spear had been in the music business for about fourteen years, and his approach had become well established.

That said, he had also become deeply dissatisfied with the way his music was promoted and marketed in Jamaica and in Europe, and the recent changes affecting Jamaican music, with the new dancehall sound becoming predominant, convinced him that the future lay elsewhere for him. So, in 1985, he moved to the USA, more precisely to Queens, NY, and set up his production company, Burning Music Production there. He moved there to be closer to his wife, Sonia Rodney, who had moved to Jamaica to be with him, but also because it made more sense from a business point of view to live there, where he would be able to market his music more easily.

1985 saw the release of *Resistance* on the Heartbeat label. The album was recorded at Tuff Gong Studio and at Aquarius Studio, with scintillating horns by David Madden, Dean Fraser, and Nambo Robinson (the Rass Brass). It is a great, militant album with three outstanding songs ("Mek We Yadd", "Holy Foundation", and "Queen of the Mountain").

"Mek We Yadd" is a rhythmical chant which makes the simple point that it is time to leave Babylon, and that in a time like this, "any man could be Babylon".

"Holy Foundation" identifies the mountains as the place of

spirituality and freedom, while "Queen of the Mountain" is a tribute to Nanny of the Maroons, the famous Maroon leader who was said to have magical powers.The song identifies Maroon culture as one of the foundations of Jamaican culture ("our livity", "our people") and includes an injunction to open the " little slave books" and "run come take a look". Three Jamaican parishes (Saint James, Saint Ann, and Saint Catherine) are singled out in the song for their historical importance. The song features a blistering guitar solo by Lenford Richards, who played on many Burning Spear records.

The title track identifies Rastafarianism and Garveyism as the twin pillars of black people's resistance as Spear reminds his audience that "the philosophy of Marcus Mosiah Garvey still lives on". "The Force" is a trance-like track that looks to Haile Selassie as the "force" driving him to higher heights.

The album closes with "Love To You", a bluesy tune with lovely guitar parts by Lenford Richards and which deals with the power of love.

Resistance was released on the Heartbeat label in America and on the Blue Moon label in France, and it certainly played its part in nurturing the reggae scene in these two countries. In New Orleans, the musician Ben E. Hunter listened keenly to this album and "Mek We Yadd" was his favourite track.

In 1986 the album entitled *People of the World* was released and introduced some changes in the personnel playing for Spear. Three female horn players are featured on the record, Jennifer Hill, Nilda Richards, and Pam Fleming. They were to play a very important part in the new sound Spear's music was to have over the next two years and were to tour with Spear. Outstanding songs on that album include "We Are Going", "This Experience" and "Distant Drum", a very moving track that echoes in the listener's mind. Another outstanding song on the *People of the World* album is "Built This City", which has a chorus similar to that of Jefferson Starship's "We Built This City", but with reggae and ska being the main musical forms referenced now.

1988 saw the release of a live album recorded at the Zenith in Paris and is a high-water mark in Spear's career. The double album confirmed that Spear was now an artist of international repute and reggae's foremost ambassador in Europe and in America.

In the same year Spear released an album that established a complete break with the past, *Mistress Music*, an album with a more modern, a brasher and livelier sound that included a lot of keyboards. Horns continued to play a central part in his music. Love and human relationships were important themes on this album with songs like "Tell The Children" ("Big, big, big embarrassment !"), "Woman I Love You", and "Say You are In Love" dealing with romantic themes like never before. Even Marcus Garvey was presented as a human being with feelings in "Love Garvey", and not as a great historical leader on a pedestal. The album raised a few eyebrows among reggae purists who thought that Burning Spear had become "Bubbling Spear", and in his review of the album for *The Beat*, Alan Ryan found it overproduced (*The Beat*, 1989). Spear was simply willing to experiment and to transcend the limitations of a purely conscious approach.

In an interview granted to Ed Paladino and published in *The Beat* in April 1989, Spear acknowledged that things had changed over the previous years and that he needed to adapt to change: "Over the past years, everything has changed, still maintaining the roots as the original Burning Spear. More people turning out and I guess more records are selling.[...]I try to prevent myself coming back to the music I will be singing from 1969 or the early 70s or late 70s, and I feel the time is right and now's the time wherein the direction what I-man looking into this day. I feel it's a good direction to create some new music, showing the people that I is the roots, and from the roots bring forth many branches and leaves" (Paladino 28). By 1989 Spear had also made important changes concerning the members of the Burning Band. The three female horn players who had become an arresting part of his shows were sacked. So were Anthony Bradshaw and Devon Bradshaw, who had played rhythm guitar and bass for Spear for years: "I want [my musicians] to be creative as much as they can be creative. But on another level, I want them to maintain the roots as close as possible, blowing the original style of Burning

Spear and phrases. This is one of the main thing why I had to get rid of the bass man. He was intent to play some different things from the original way. And what caused the changes, we been to Africa on a Sunsplash level and it was his first time seeing Sly and Robbie playing together and he believe in patterning Robbie by doing Robbie do and I realize that Taxi sound is not Burning sound and Burning sound is not Taxi sound. So no way you can play Taxi sound for Burning Spear, you working for Burning Spear, you have to play Burning Spear sound, and he get carried away and he start to play everything different. And that was one of the main reasons why I have to get rid of the bass man. So, it's like we been to Europe and doing a seven-week tour and I have to fire them in Hamburg -that's where I sent them back home- both of them... brothers. The tour finished in London and I didn't take back the girls, and let them know that they're out" (Paladino 29).

The 1990s opened with the release of a new album (*Mek We Dweet*) and marked Spear's return to Island. The sound on that album was dominated by horn hooks and great electric guitar solos with at times a more hurried pace, but Spear's preoccupations remained the same. On "My Roots", he says that he will never forget his roots and the "road [he] has travelled" and this album proves it. The track entitled "Elephants" is a kind of parable in which Spear takes elephants' willingness to stand together and to defend one another as a model for African unity: he thus encourages African nations to unite. In an interview he granted to the *Los Angeles Times* journalist Jim Washburn, Spear explained the context to the writing of that song: " 'Elephants' came about when I was traveling in West Africa," he said, "It was my first time ever seeing elephants. They were at the river, and when we tried to go close to them, they were all backing up on each other, defending each other. If mankind could really see that and exercise it, you'd see how close people would get, by just looking at the elephant. Now is the time when you have to live like the elephant to live in Africa--get closer."(Jim Washburn, "A Reggae Mission : For Burning Spear, Whose Tour Is Coming to Irvine, Music Is Vehicle for Love, Understanding", *The Los Angeles Times*, June 1, 1990).

To promote the album, Rodney toured the USA as part of the

Reggae Sunsplash Tour, which also featured Freddie McGregor, Marcia Griffiths, Shinehead, Shelly Thunder, and U-Roy.

"Garvey" paid tribute to his Saint Ann parishmate, and "Great Men" was a tribute to Paul Bogle, Marcus Garvey, Nelson Mandela, Malcolm X, Martin Luther King and other great black leaders. The guitar solo by Lenford Richards is particularly effective on that didactic track which functions as a praise song for black leaders.

Jah Kingdom came out in 1991 and was recorded at Grove Music recording studio in Ocho Rios. It is quite a mellow album with a warm sound and sophisticated arrangements. The album is notable for its inclusion of a track Spear had recorded for a Grateful Dead tribute album, a version of Jerry Garcia's "Estimated Prophet". Spear had been contacted by Garcia about taking part in that tribute album, and he had accepted as he had grown to like the Grateful Dead and their trance-like and spaced-out music, which in a way was similar to his own. He had gone to a couple of their concerts and had enjoyed the experience.

In his review of the album for *The Washington Post*, Mike Joyce noted that the album did not present anything new, but that Rodney's "soulful" voice and "economical phrasing" carried the day as his voice was strong enough to make any material interesting ("As always, it isn't what Rodney sings that counts, it's how he sings it."). Joyce also commented on the rock and pop elements that had been introduced to make Spear's music more accessible to an American audience. Indeed, Spear had been living in the USA for quite a few years by then and had established a fan base there. The release of the *Jah Kingdom* album was followed by a tour to promote the album.

1993 saw the release of *The World Should Know,* an album recorded at Grove Studio in Ocho Rios, Jamaica, and mixed in New York at Platinum Island Studio. The musicians who played on this album included Robbie Lyn on keyboards, Nelson Miller (Spear's long-time friend) on drums, Lenford Richards on guitar, as well as Nambo Robinson, Chico Chin, and Dean Fraser on trombone, trumpet, and saxophone respectively. Barry O'Hare was the sound engineer and gave the album a bright and warm sound. The album was nominated for a Best Reggae Album award.

The title track finds Spear tackling the themes of equality and justice as he bemoans the fact that resources are unequally shared and he asks the questions "Why should one man want it all?".

On the upbeat tune "Identity" Spear plainly states that he will not change his identity musically and that "Jah works must be done". Other cultural tunes include "It's Not a Crime" and "I Stand Strong", but the album also includes a few love songs or at least songs that could be called "romantic" ("What A Lovin' Day" and "Sweeter Than Chocolate"). In fact, as pointed out by Jo-Ann Greene in her review of the album, the album can be said to fall into two parts: a cultural chapter, and a more varied set of songs, with tunes about love or music. What makes the album distinctive is its use of more modern, danceable beats, probably a nod to the dancehall phenomenon that was taking Jamaica by storm then. That probably got Spear his Grammy nomination.

In 1995 Spear released *Rasta Business*, an album which was recorded at Grove Recording Studio in Ocho Rios, and which was given a modern sound by Barry O'Hare. The title track establishes a clear distinction between fashion-obsessed "funky dreads" and the "real" Rastas ("Rasta business") while "Not Stupid" makes its point very powerfully and references Spear's "Slavery Days" in the process. By then, Spear was quoting from his own songs and this is an endearing aspect of his music.

On "Subject In School", Spear pleads for the inclusion of Garveyite studies on school curricula, a theme he was to come back to repeatedly. "Legal Hustlers" is a dig at the people who exploit Jamaican music for their own personal ends ("riding on reggae bandwagon"). On "This Man", Spear delivers a series of powerful messages about the "small people" exploited by "politicians" and claims that "anyone could be Babylon". In other words, the system is corrupt, not individuals. The hypnotic backing track and sweet harmonies complement Spear's insights nicely.

In 1997 *Appointment With His Majesty* was released and contained outstanding tracks like "Play Jerry", his tribute to Jerry

Garcia, the lead singer of The Grateful Dead, "Reggae Physician", "My Island" and "Commercial Development". Rodney had been contacted by Jerry Garcia in 1991 to find out whether he would agree to contribute to a project he was supervising entitled *Deadicated*, and he had covered Garcia's "Estimated Prophet" for that album. Rodney had by then become a fan of The Grateful Dead's music and on "Play Jerry", he described the peculiar atmosphere at a Grateful Dead concert.

One of the strongest tracks on the album is probably "Don't Sell Out" on which Spear is accompanied only by percussions and guitars, a format which brings to mind Bob Marley's "Redemption Songs". Spear encourages Caribbean people to remain faithful to their roots and he mentions the "afro-slave yards" of the past but also the "teachers", "farmers", "doctors", and "nurses" of the present time. This song is a kind of paean to Caribbean people, but, as Spear insisted in an interview granted to the *Beat* journalist Carter Van Pelt, it was not directed at Jamaica: " "Don't Sell Out" is universal. It's not like the song base up on Jamaica, dealing with Jamaica people and Jamaica politicians. It's not like that. This song is an open song. It can be any island. It can be any country. It can be any place. There are so many places today selling out" (Carter Van Pelt, *The Beat*, Vol. 17 #1, 1998). In fact this song had been released on Spear's own Rasta Business imprint in the summer of 1996, and it had been the first in years that Spear's music had been available in Jamaica.

Other tracks on the album address similar themes, like for instance "My Island" and "Commercial Development". The development of tourism and the risks this implies for Jamaican culture and for the environment are major themes in these songs, and he even likens these developments to the acts perpetrated by Christopher Columbus and seventeenth-century pirates.

On "My Island" he sends a clear warning to those who live in Jamaica and buy property there without contributing to the development of the island and promises to wage a "musical" war on them: "Music is more than just listening. People use the music for them protection at times... So is not like a physical fight. It's not like we're going out there to go hit nobody with fists or anything like that. It's more like an intelligent fight, educational fight, musical fight" (Van Pelt, 1998).

"African Jamaican" relates an incident which happened to Spear when he was stopped and searched by customs officials in Jamaica as he was "going back home". He saw the sign "Nothing to Declare" and assumed that he would be allowed to go through, but he had to submit to a search. As an expatriate living in America, Spear was looking at developments in Jamaica and he did not like what he saw: "Many times I going back to Jamaica, I been hassled … without a cause. I can remember some time, me and one of my sons was going down. And they got this big sign "Nothing to Declare". And my bags were so small, so I thinking that this is the correct line to go in, 'cause I don't have anything to declare. And this officer would stop me and would take my bag and … get it searched, and all these people would pass with three, four suitcases – people they classify to be tourist or foreigner or guest … I'm not against tourists or foreigners or guests. It just bothers I to know that I'm an African-Jamaican born in Jamaica, live in Jamaica, still do business in Jamaica, still spending back money in the country. They don't care who you is... what kind of upliftment you do for the island or country. They're dealing with rules and regulations and laws and principles, but overall for everyone. And sometime that really hurt. It's not like I'm the only person that really take place with. Some of those people been hassled more than I've been hassled" (Van Pelt, 1998).

The title track bemoans the rising crime rate and the violence which were engulfing Jamaica then ("Every day me say gun a-fire") and establishes a parallel with new musical developments ("We want back the roots and the music").

 A couple of lighter and danceable tracks ("Reggae Physician", "Music", and "Loving You") rounded off this upbeat and modern-sounding album which garnered Spear his second Grammy nomination.

In 1999 *Calling Rastafari* was released and this was the album that finally got Burning Spear his first Grammy Award. The album opens with the autobiographical "As It Is", which updates Spear's own "No One Remembers Old Marcus Garvey" with the new chorus "Did someone remember Burning Spear?". Spear reminisces about his struggle to make it in the music business and about the time when he travelled from Saint Ann's Bay to "13 Brentford Road" to audition for Clement Dodd at Studio One: "That song came about because I was still in the whole Jamaican thing where there was this kind of environment where people weren't respecting Spear and this whole new kind of music was dominating the scene. Since then, on another level, I have come to realize that people will always remember I and my work. I feel good about it. I've made my mark. I've done the right thing as I feel I should have done it. I have listened to Jah and got the work done" (Doug Heselgrave, "Positive: An Interview With Burning Spear", *United Reggae*, April 2012)..

One of the outstanding tracks on the album is the one entitled "Statue of Liberty" in which Spear recalls that America "stretched forth her hands" to welcome many immigrants who came to work in hospitals, as cleaners or in agriculture, but now things seem to have changed and he is asking her to "light up" her torch so that the people can see.

Conscious and message-laden songs are in order here, with for instance "Let's Move", which recycles the traditional song "Brown Girl in a Ring".

"You Want Me To" finds Spear in a lovers mood and the sound on that track certainly recalls British Lovers Rock as Spear croons about going on a sea cruise with his lover. "House of Reggae" is a tribute to the power of reggae music, with a reference to Marcus Garvey's " African legendary parades" to make sure that the foundations of the music are not forgotten.

Freeman was released in 2003, on Spear's Burning Music label, which was proof of his constant efforts to control as much as possible every aspect of music production, from the recording of albums to the marketing of his "products" and the booking of his tours. By 2003, Spear had established a viable business enterprise and was in control of many aspects of his career. His wife, Sonia Rodney, had been a key part of this enterprise for the last 15 years and was in charge of booking his shows and promoting his music (Van Pelt, *The Beat*, 2004). Spear had parted company with

Heartbeat Records who had released all his albums since the early 1980s, starting with *Farover*. There was no acrimony in this parting but it was simply a shrewd business move.

The album was recorded at Harry J's studio, and featured the musicianship of Leroy "Horsemouth" Wallace for the first time in many years, Uzziah "Sticky" Thomson, and Chris Meredith.

This album was a return to form, so to speak with hard-hitting tracks like "Trust", "Old School", and "Not Guilty". "Old School" pleads for a return to traditional values in the music business, and "Not Guilty" references all the great heroes of the black cause like Marcus Garvey, Malcom X ("the American Marcus Garvey") and Martin Luther King. As had been customary for Spear for a number of years by then, he was now referencing his own musical legacy and quoting from his own songs, as for instance with "We Feel It", whose opening sends the listener back to "Marcus Children Suffer", the first track on the *Social Living* album. Likewise "Ha Ha"'s opening quotes the first lines from Spear's own "Shout It Out".

On "Changes", Spear warns world leaders that sometimes they have to adapt to change and that "two wrongs cannot make one right", while "Rock and Roll" happily mixes reggae and rock, with some blistering guitar solos.

On the horn-driven "Rise Up", Spear pays tribute to Marcus Garvey, who rose up from his "little island", the same island Bob Marley came from.

2005 saw the release of *Our Music* on Spear's own Burning Music label. The album was recorded in New York, at the Magic Shop Studio with Barry O'Hare as sound engineer and featured strong cultural tracks like "Our Music", which dealt with record companies' attitude towards reggae music ("Not selling, not selling, not selling !") and 'Down in Jamaica". Uplifting tunes like "Try Again". "Little Garvey" and "One Marcus" sang the praises of Rodney's hero, Marcus Garvey, whose name has to be cleared, Spear insists, since he was wrongfully accused. The track entitled "Together" is a plea for peace and unity which quotes from two Burning Spear songs, "Bad to Worse" and "Throw Down Your Arms".

In 2008 Spear released *Jah Is Real,* an album which was recorded in New York at the Magic Shop studio and which provided Spear with his second Grammy award. The sound is bright and modern, with rock-influenced guitar lines and hard-hitting horn parts. The album is also notable for featuring collaborations with the bassist Bootsy Collins and the keyboard player Bernie Worrell, both well-known for being members of the P-Funk band Parliament Funkadelic. This was a deliberate attempt at broadening Spear's sound and making the album different from his previous efforts. As Spear explained: "We never compromise where the music itself is concerned, but between my wife and I, we sit down thinking about what we could do to make this album special, to make it different from the rest. We go over a lot of things before we decide what we're going to do, because if you notice, we bring in a couple of guys who never get to play with Burning Spear yet, and we come up with some strong ideas regarding the arrangements. We make it well frothy and catchy and then when we drop it, it was like, "Wow ! It was *smooth* !" (Masouri, *Echoes*, April 2009). Bootsie Collins and Bernie Worrell ended up playing on tracks like "People in High Places", "Step It", and "You Were Wrong", but they did not set out to change Spear's sound. In fact these tracks sound and feel like reggae tunes. In fact, the two Parliament Funkadelic stalwarts got on really well with Spear.

Jah Is Real features some tracks on which Spear settled a few accounts with the music business. On "Wickedness", he takes record companies to task for exploiting Jamaican artists and for failing to pay them any decent royalties, and on "Run For Your Life", he laments the fact that the music business has changed and that things are not the way they used to be. On "No Compromise", Spear insists that his music is "never-looking-back music", and that he's "never looking back", always forward.

After the release of *Jah Is Real*, Spear went into semi-retirement, but continued to tour. One of his last concerts was in Nairobi, where he played in a stadium in front of 80,000 people. Work on a new album started around 2010 (*No Destroyer*) but only gave birth to a single ("Mommy") which was eventually released in 2021.

Burning Spear stopped touring around 2014 as he no longer had the energy to launch into worldwide tours, and the Covid pandemic put an end to touring for many recording artistes anyway. Then during the pandemic, conspiracy theories about vaccination began to spread on social media and on the internet, and the Jamaican cultural icon Sizzla even released a tune entitled "No Vaccine". Spear then courageously spoke about this double-vaccination status during an interview which was broadcast on the radio station WPKN in April 2021: "It meant a lot to me as an old guy, where something went wrong in another country and it reach up to where you live, and they come up with protection that you can protect yourself from getting that virus, so I became part of that plan" (Katz 2022).

The end of the pandemic led to Spear's return to touring, with the first tour in many years slotted for 2022. In August 2022 he performed in Birmingham (UK) and London, for the first time in seventeen years.

The *No Destroyer* album was eventually released in August 2023 on his Burning Spear Music label. The album features message-laden tracks like "Cure For Cancer", which encourages governments to devote more money to medical research instead of their defence budgets and "Jamaica", which insists on Jamaica's contribution to world culture, with reggae and the Rastafarian religion or lifestyle ("livity" as the Rastas would say). Other tracks on the album like the title track, "They Think", "No Fool", and "Obsession" pit Spear against the recording industry and bemoan the treatment he has received from the major labels over the years. Spear calls them "sharks" and claims that they have tried to destroy him and to derail his career. The track entitled "Independent" leaves no doubt as to the price Burning Spear has paid for the cultural and financial independence he has tried to conquer ever since he started working as a recording artiste.

II
Studio One Presents Burning Spear: The Birth of a Rasta Reggae Legend
(David Bousquet)

To many fans and critics, Burning Spear's career truly began in 1975 when Winston Rodney initiated his collaboration with Ocho Rios producer Jack Ruby. The album *Marcus Garvey* and its dub version *Garvey's Ghost*, especially, are often thought to be Burning Spear's breakthrough pieces, establishing his unique style. Despite Rodney's dissatisfaction with Island's alterations to his music, the deal with Chris Blackwell's production company on these albums and the subsequent *Man In The Hills* helped Burning Spear reach wide audiences internationally. Since then, he has become one of the greatest reggae legends of all time.

Yet, Rodney's career started as early as 1969 when he met Sir Clement Coxsone Dodd, the founder and owner of legendary Studio One. According to some, Rodney had sought advice from no other than Bob Marley himself about starting a career in the music business, as both men came from St Ann's Bay. Yet, as is often the case in the history of Jamaican music, others also claim the paternity of Rodney's first encounter with Dodd, notably engineer and arranger Larry Marshall. What is certain is that Burning Spear ended up auditioning for Dodd at Brentford Road and went on to record a series of groundbreaking singles at Studio One. Most of this material also features on two albums comprising Rodney's early work: *Studio One Presents Burning Spear* (1973) and *Rocking Time* (1974)·

In those days, Burning Spear was still the name of Rodney's band, alternatively mentioned on some record labels as The Burning Spears. Their first single, the classic "Door Peeper" from 1969 (also known as "Door Peep Shall Not Enter"), featured Rodney as lead vocalist with bass singer Rupert Willington. They were later joined by tenor Delroy Hinds, with whom they would record most of their material for both Dodd and Ruby. As all

Studio One singers of the time, Burning Spear recorded with Dodd's dream team of musicians known as Sound Dimension. It featured Jackie Mittoo on keyboards, Leroy Sibbles on bass, Bunny Williams on drums, Roland Alphonso and Cedric Brooks on saxophone, as well as a myriad of other talented players of instruments who stopped by Brentford Road every so often for a session.

Burning Spear's Studio One material is remarkable in many ways. It is quite typical of the early reggae era, with prominent organ riffs, faster tempos and an even heavier emphasis on the electric bass than in the previous rocksteady period. Compared to earlier Studio One productions, these songs have a less polished, rougher sound that came to be so appreciated by fans around the world and notably by the English skinheads. Yet Burning Spear was one of the few artists recorded by Dodd in the early seventies who pioneered the roots music of the second half of the decade. Together with The Abyssinians and Horace Andy, Rodney emerged as an openly Rasta singer with a radical and uncompromising message of Black emancipation. As pointed out by Steve Barrow and Peter Dalton in their *Rough Guide to Reggae*, it is likely that this aspect of Spear's music was less appealing to white British teenagers than other Studio One productions of the same period. Ultimately, though, it would provide the foundation of Spear's popularity in the years and decades to come.

Indeed, Burning Spear's Studio One productions already display all the unique characteristics of his music. Rodney actually recorded new versions of many of these songs later in his career, and some of them have formed the backbone of his setlist until today for the extraordinary live performances he is so famous for. Despite their raw character, the Studio One versions are seminal and as enjoyable as their later incarnations. As Barrow and Dalton remind us, "it says something about his artistry that it is impossible to choose between the raw originals on these two sets and the more 'produced' later versions" (Barrow and Dalton 93).

In musical terms, the twenty-four songs recorded for Dodd feature heavy-bass early reggae riddims where harmonic progression is kept to a bare minimum. Unlike the sweetness of rocksteady tunes, this music is rough and tough with a sound nearing distortion on many songs. Rodney's singing is almost off tune on a couple of recordings, adding to the overall atmosphere of haziness and tension. While a few songs feature instrumental passages, mainly on the saxophone, they mostly serve to reinforce the percussive quality of the riddims and are quite remote from the jazzy improvisations of ska or the melodic sophistication of rocksteady. These tunes are also testimonies of the first sound experimentations of dub engineers, with a number of psychedelic effects like the fuzzy guitar of "Foggy Road" or the reverb-full ending of "Pick Up The Pieces". "Joe Frazier" also offers a dubbed reinterpretation of "He Prayed", where the vocal and instrumental tracks are sometimes muted. Many of these singles were in fact released with a dub version on the B-side.

This kind of production, on top of being typical of the changes that occurred in Jamaican music at the dawn of the seventies, is also quite fitting to showcase Rodney's unique singing style. This is perhaps Burning Spear's most characteristic and memorable musical innovation, as many of the songs do not feature a traditional alternation between verse and chorus but are rather based on a repetitive and hypnotic structure that accompanies Rodney's vocal incantations. The lyrics do not fall into regular, binary patterns and the words often do not rhyme. Spear seems to improvise his singing and let inspiration drive his rhythmic syncopations and melodic convolutions, much as he does in his extended live performances of the songs.

These early records are clearly influenced by the late rhythm 'n' blues and southern soul sounds from the US, but Rodney also goes back much further in time to revive the deep spirituality of Black church hymns. As one of the first Rasta singers to record music in Jamaica, he also borrows from the Burru and Nyabinghi drumming styles played during reasoning sessions and groundations in the ghettoes of Kingston. Spear's Studio One material counts among the first records to introduce these musical elements, which would eventually make their way into the reggae mainstream later in the decade.

This musical landscape provides the perfect background for Spear to deliver his incendiary message. While many of the classic tunes produced during the early reggae era retained the romantic themes of rocksteady or showcased the rough masculinity and aggression of the Kingston rude boys, Rodney's twenty-odd songs for Studio One offer an almost exclusively Rasta rebel content, focusing on Black emancipation and empowerment. Perhaps the best example of this is Spear's very first record, "Door Peep" from 1969. It opens on an acappella intro where Rodney firmly declares his faith in Rastafari. This is also an opportunity for him to establish his name, "Burning Spear" being a reference to a military award created by Jomo Kenyatta, the first president of Kenya as it became independent from British rule. Rastafarians were deeply influenced by the Mau Mau uprising of the late fifties in Kenya, which ultimately led to the country's independence in 1963. The Mau Mau warriors notably refused to cut their hair until their fight for freedom was over, and the pictures that made it to Jamaica through the British press inspired Rastafarians to grow their famous dreadlocks as a symbol of their African ancestry and pride. Spears also feature on the Kenyan flag. The rest of "Door Peep" is an invitation to "give thanks and praise" and "chant down Babylon", establishing some of the imagery and phraseology that would be heard so many times in subsequent reggae productions.

A predominant theme in these songs is that of movement and mobility, making Rodney one these "travelling men" that populate reggae music but also the imaginary of the African diaspora more generally ("Travelling Man" is a 1974 song by Dennis Brown. One of Burning Spear's classics from 1975 is also entitled "Travelling"). There is an obvious reference there to the exodus of Black people and their deportation from Africa, as in "Journey" or "Foggy Road", whose titles are quite evocative. These lyrics are calls for Black people to remember their history, a theme close to Rodney's heart which he would take up on the classic "Slavery Days" for instance. In "Creation" and "He Prayed", Spear portrays himself as a loner journeying along a forgotten road, despised and mocked by everyone, using a figure a theme often found in the blues. The Creation Rebel, then, is also a prophet who can clearly see the fate of his people while many remain blind to the destiny that awaits them. As such, he denounces the poverty and misery that plague his community, a typical Rasta theme that appears in "Bad to Worst" for example. As a righteous Rastaman, Rodney is entitled to speak for his community but he also does not hesitate to castigate those who err on the way, as in "Weeping And Wailing".

Yet, these songs are also reminders for Spear's listeners not to give up in the face of adversity. Despite the hardships and tribulations, better days will come and Rodney makes sure to celebrate the impending revelation that is synonymous with liberation. Africans were able to survive in the New World, as recalled in "Ethiopians Live It Out", and a bright future will await them once they will recognise the glory of Rastafari, as mentioned in "Foggy Road". Songs like "We Are Free" or "What A Happy Day" celebrate the joy of emancipation in a manner that resembles the gospel anthems of the Black churches of the south of the US. This can take the form of a symbolic repatriation to the African homeland, as in "Call On You". "Get Ready" also makes use of the image of the train on which Black people must jump to go back home, which is a frequent reference in the US soul music of the 1960s. This song might be a specific reference to "People Get Ready" from 1965 by The Impressions, which would be covered by Bob Marley with "One Love/People Get Ready" the same year before being recorded again for Island on the album *Exodus* in 1977 and becoming an international hit.

Overall, these songs encourage Black people to know themselves and acknowledge where they come from. This will give them a new sense of pride and confidence and lead them on the road to racial emancipation, as stated in "This Race" and "Rocking Time". "Swell Headed" emphasises Spear's tenacity and resilience, not losing faith despite the obstacles along the way, themes that are also incidentally evoked through the figure of famous African American boxer Joe Frazier. They will thus eventually reach the promised land, Mount Zion in Rasta parlance, as evoked by Spear in "Zion Higher", and create a "New Civilization". In "This Population", Rodney's tone makes itself less prophetic and biblical to demand very concrete change for the Afro-Jamaican masses in the form of schools, trade centres and industries, thus calling for the economic development of the island. By the early seventies, the dream of independence had turned into a nightmare for many Black Jamaicans as the promises of the new postcolonial political elites had failed to materialise. As poverty and violence became the order of the day, a sense of rebellion resurfaced which echoed the turmoil that agitated the African continent and the diaspora throughout the sixties. By the end of the decade, the mood was no longer about celebration and entertainment and the time was ripe for more radical voices such as Spear's to emerge in the Jamaican music industry.

In this very consistent set of religious and political calls for action, a few songs stand out that focus on romantic themes. "Don't Mess With Jill", for instance, has a fairly stereotypical lyric stating Rodney's jealousy regarding the object of his affection and is certainly of one his less memorable efforts of his Studio One period. In the same vein, "Girls Like You" provides a fairly paternalistic portrait of women as figures of deception, who are denounced as such by the figure of the righteous Rastaman, in a manner probably inspired by biblical episodes. It is striking to see though how Spear couches this unfortunately common theme in Jamaican music in religious language. Despite its title, "Down By The Riverside" is also a song that deals with Rodney's affection for a girl whom he enjoins not to break his heart. Interestingly, the lyrics still subtly allude to a sense Black identity that stretches across the African diaspora as Spear cannot decide whether the woman he loves is Jamaican, American or African.

"Mamie" and "Old Time Sayin" deal with the theme of family, another typical element in the music and literature of the New World Blacks, although their precise meaning remains somewhat hard to decipher. They both stage maternal figures and state the importance of the unconditional love one receives from one's mother. But they also dwell on the importance of the past, which one cannot change nor erase, and on the themes of authority and punishment. "Pick Up The Pieces", one of Spear's timeless classics, evokes a metaphorical cleaning or cleansing which might be interpreted as a call for Black people to collect themselves and find the true meaning of Rastafari. In "Them A Come", Spear witnesses a large and diverse crowd gathering and running, although the ultimate meaning of this image remains unclear. As many other Jamaican songs, "Fire Down Below" makes use of a popular proverb and stages Spear as a teapot ready to boil over, perhaps an image of the impending revolution to come.

While the precise meaning of this last group of songs remains quite cryptic, they contribute to the apocalyptic atmosphere that characterises Burning Spear's early work for Studio One and that became a trademark of his musical career. The combination of the dry and heavy early reggae riddims played by Sound Dimension and Spear's prophetic lyrics and trance-inducing lyrics makes these recordings part of the most striking and unique of this era of Jamaican music. While Clement Dodd was often criticised for being more commercially than musically driven, one can only acknowledge his understanding of the audiences' appetites and of the emerging trends in the music business. Coxsone was the only producer at the time to welcome Rasta artists in his studio, and without his flair neither Burning Spear's career nor the international explosion of roots reggae in the mid seventies would have been possible.

Spear's recordings at Studio One are impossible to overlook for anyone claiming to be his fan, nor in fact for any self-respecting reggae lover. These songs were played by some of the best Jamaican musicians of all time and recorded in the most iconic of Kingston's studios, and they are sung by one of the most unique and legendary voices in reggae music. As Burning Spear is making his comeback on stage and on record, one can only celebrate his first efforts as some of the best Jamaican music ever. The pioneering character of these songs makes Spear a true prophet, at least in terms of his musical achievements. One can listen to these songs over and over again without ever getting bored, and relish in the many later live and studio versions that make his music so rich and fascinating. As Walter Rodney keeps reinventing himself, his heritage will live through the ages and continue to inspire new generations of fans and musicians. May the Spear burn forever!

III
Burning Spear's Self-Productions:
Keep The Spear Burning
(James Danino)

In Jamaica the recording industry has always operated somewhat differently to those of other countries. Though similarly to everywhere else there are what one might call "major labels", what sets Jamaica apart is that from early in its development, there have been numerous small producers, labels and record companies. This may be in part due to the fact that the record industry in Jamaica started as a fairly informal sector.

Ken Khouri is widely credited with having been the first man to import a cutting lathe and to have started a small-scale recording and "soft-wax" cutting business. Around 1944, while on a trip to Miami, he was having his car radio fixed and the mechanic happened to mention that he owned a machine that could record from a microphone straight onto disc. Khouri, being a curious man and having sufficient funds, offered to buy the machine and took it back to Jamaica. Initially he thought of it more of as a an interesting gadget than a money-making prospect, and it was only when someone at a party suggested that he might use the machine to record the Calypsos being performed live at nightclubs that it started to become the basis for a business. Indeed, he was the first man in Jamaica to record Jamaican music for resale and after having secured a partnership with a shop called Times Store he began recording, pressing and selling Jamaican music. The business quickly flourished and became Federal Studios and Pressing Plant.

From these serendipitous beginnings, many other people decided to get in on the idea of recording music made locally and pressing and selling records made in Jamaica. Big companies such as WIRL (West Indian Record Label), Studio One, Treasure Isle, Giant and Prince Buster to name a few became some of the front-runners in the industry.

Recording and pressing being a relatively costly enterprise, most of these companies were run by reasonably well-off individuals. Despite this, as early as the 1960s, smaller and less wealthy individuals also decided to try and get in on the burgeoning record industry in a variety of ways. Some producers did not own studios and would rent studio time for their recording sessions at one of the established studios and would then take care of having the recording mastered, pressed and distributed in Jamaica and abroad.

Eventually, some of the artists themselves, though they were often in difficult financial situations, also decided to try their hand at producing and selling their own records.

There were multiple reasons for this. One of the main reasons is that, generally speaking, artists were not well paid for their recordings by the bigger producers and were basically told that if they were not happy about it they could go elsewhere.

A secondary reason was that there were a great number of singers trying to become professional artists and so there was a lot of competition to face before being chosen by a producer and given a chance to record a song or more for them. This led to talented artists being rejected by producers and unable to secure recording deals. This state if affairs led some of them who believed that they had what it took to make it, to raise funds to produce their own songs. They would rent studio time, employ session musicians and engineers and try their hardest to sing a song that would allow them to at least recoup the money they had invested. In the best case scenario they would be able to make some money and attract the attention of some of the bigger producers with established labels. These artists would often set up record labels of their own to release their music. In this case the term "record label" is used in its loosest possible definition because, more often than not, these labels had no physical premises, no capital and where little more than a name and a label design to be imprinted on the records themselves. Most of the time, these artist-run labels did not have the necessary funds for things like pressing large numbers of records and after having pressed a small first batch would attempt to have them distributed by more established distributors and labels. If these distributors thought the song had potential, they might press more copies and thus give the song a better chance of widespread play and sales in Jamaica and abroad.

There are many examples of artists who have since become famous internationally having tried this method. Perhaps the most famous example of this is Bob Marley and the Wailers. After having worked at Studio One and become dissatisfied with the returns they were obtaining from Clement Dodd despite high numbers of sales, they decided to launch the Wailn N Soul M and Tuff Gong record label in order to be in control of the whole process. Theoretically it is a great idea, but the Wailers were soon confronted with the realities of the record industry. Indeed, it is one thing to be able to raise the funds necessary to record and press a small number of records, it is quite another to be able to have those songs played by the sound systems, sold in the record shops and distributed internationally to a wider audience. Though the Wail N Soul M productions undeniably had the needed quality, the label found it hard to make sufficient funds to make a living for all of the members of the Wailers. It can be argued that this is one of the main reasons that the Wailers went on to work with Danny Sims of Jad Records, Lee Perry and ultimately Chris Blackwell of Island Records. Neither Sims nor Perry were able to break them into the mainstream international market, but Blackwell, having established his Island Records company with international hits like "My Boy Lollipop" by Millie Small, had the funds, connections and structure that was necessary to take the Wailers from a successful but poor Jamaican group with hits to an international hit-making group.

Two of the three original members, Peter Tosh and Bunny Wailer, dissatisfied with the direction they were going and their positions in the group after the release of the second album Burnin, decided to start solo careers. Interestingly, all three of the original members went on to form their own record labels with Peter Tosh setting up Intel Diplo, Bunny Wailer creating Solomonic and Bob Marley developing the Tuff Gong label.

It is worth noting that Burning Spear got into recording after having met Bob Marley in the mid-1960s and Marley suggesting to the group, at the time comprised of Winston Rodney and Rupert Willingston, that they should go to Studio One and audition there.

After having followed Marley's advice and having passed the audition, the group recorded some of its most memorable and long-lasting music at Studio One. Similarly to the Wailers, Burning Spear became unhappy with the treatment they received at the hands of Clement Dodd and decided to stop working for him. Though Winston Rodney and Rupert Willingston had fallen out after recording a dozen or so tracks at Studio One, they got back together and added Delroy Hinds as a harmony singer when they began to record what was to become one of Burning Spear's most important albums, *Marcus Garvey* for producer Jack Ruby. This album caught the attention of Chris Blackwell's Island records and a deal was struck that lead to it being released internationally and becoming one of Jamaican music's most well known and best selling albums of all time. A second album, *Man in The Hills*, was recorded with Jack Ruby and also met with considerable success and international recognition.

Despite this success, the group did not continue recording for Jack Ruby, and Winston Rodney split from the the two other members of the trio and the name Burning Spear came to be associated with Winston Rodney alone.

There is one notable exception to this statement, During the time of the recording of these two albums with Jack Ruby, Rupert Willingston recorded a song entitled "See Dem Da" with members of the group but not including Winston Rodney and this song was released credited to Rupert Wellington [sic], Burning Spear. It is the the only known instance of a song credited to Burning Spear as group that does not include Winston Rodney and on which Rupert Willingston sings as lead vocalist. The song did not meet with great success and was released on the short lived Jah Marcus Roots label with production credit attributed to Winston McKenzie, based in New York.

It is during this same period that Winston Rodney launched the Spear record label. This name is the first appearance of a record label and production company run by Winston Rodney. Indeed, though there have been a variety of names it would seem that Spear, Burning Spear, Marcus Music and Rasta Business are simply different names for the same production company and record label owned by Winston Rodney.

As was the case with other artists, it is clearly to have more control over his music and to reap a bigger proportion of the fruits of his labour that Burning Spear decided to launch his own label.

Burning Spear launched the first version of his label "Spear" in 1975 with two singles that did not appear on the studio albums he was working on at the time with Jack Ruby. Both feature instrumentals made by Phillip Fullwood, a percussionist and cousin of George "Fully" Fullwood.

The first of these singles, "Travelling", is a new version of the song entitled "Journey" which had been recorded at Studio One. Following that, "Free" was released the same year. Both of these songs and Phillip Fullwood's versions were later compiled on the Pressure Sounds *Spear Burning* compilation.

"Free" was initially released on "Spear" in 1975, but was also released the following year in 1976 on the Total Sounds label and retitled "Free Black People". In 1980 It was re-released as "Whole World Want to Be Free" on the "Burning Spear" label as a twelve-inch, this time with horn overdubs and a different mix. This twelve-inch was licensed to the "Tribesman" label in the UK, run by the producer and sound system owner Lloyd Coxsone. The song relates the history and desire for freedom of black people in Jamaica and more generally all black people who are descended from the slaves taken from Africa to work in the West. Both versions of this twelve-inch single are highly sought-after collector's itemsd with the "Burning Spear" label issue being the most sought after of the two.

At some point, Burning Spear, in collaboration with Tuff Gong records, released pressings of the *Marcus Garvey* album produced by Jack Ruby. Over time this album has been pressed on fifty-two separate occasions and it is unclear at what stage Burning Spear released it on his own label. It is fairly common for producers in Jamaica to allow artists that have their own label to press music that the artist did not produce. In some cases that was the only payment the payment the artists got: a stamper or a tape which would allow them to press and sell copies and keep the money they made from these copies.

1976 saw the release of four singles on the "Spear" imprint. "Spear Burning" was released as a single that was not included on future albums and subsequently gave its name to the compilation released by Pressure Sounds.

"The Youth" is a remake of "Pick Up The Pieces" that he originally sang at Studio One. It was first released in 1976 on a 45, and does not appear on any studio album though it has become a staple of Spear's live performances.

In 1978 "The Youth" was re-released on the Burning Spear label as a twelve-inch, coupled with "The Sun" on the AA side, it is another remake of a Studio One classic. This twelve-inch was pressed in the United States and has become a rare and pricey collector's item.

Also released are the two first records that are not Burning Spear material. "Love Everyone" by Phillip Fullwood recycles the rhythm track used on Spear's song "Free" and features Fullwood on vocals. This track also appears on a short-lived label named Free that released four Phillip Fullwood songs.

1976 also saw the release of "On That Day" as seven-inch single, which seems to be the only song sung by Burning Jr.

The year 1977 saw three singles released as well as the pressing of the *Dry And Heavy* and *Live* albums produced by Island Records. It would seem Burning Spear negotiated an arrangement for pressing rights of these albums for releases destined for the Jamaican market. The *Live* album seems to be the first instance of a record appearing on the "Burning Spear" label which features more detailed artwork and the trademark deep blue backdrop. The *Dry and Heavy* albums includes "The Sun", a reworking of the Studio One era "Call On You" which was released the following year on the aforementioned twelve-inch single.

Also included on the *Dry and Heavy* album is "Thrown Down Your Arms" which was released in 1977 as a seben-inch single on the Spear imprint. Interestingly the B side dub version is called "I

Long To See You". The song has come to be one of Burning Spear's classics and is loved by fans across the world.

The twelve-inch single "Institution" is a reworking of the Studio One track "He Prayed" also known as "Joe Frazier". This twelve-inch features a discomix dub and a full B side dub version.

Also released as a twelve-inch, a format that was gaining popularity at the time is "I Am He", sung by The Jomos. This group is named after Jomo Kenyatta the revolutionary fighter who became the first president of Kenya. Winston Rodney was inspired to take the name Burning Spear as that is the literal meaning of"Jomo" in the Kikuyu language. This song is one of only two releases by the Jomos, both appearing on Burning Spear labels.

By the end of the 1970s Burning Spear had become a well-established international touring artist but he continued to release singles and pressings of albums produced by other labels on his own label in Jamaica destined for the local market.

1978 was no different and that year he released three singles as well as a pressing of the *Live* album and a pressing of the *Social Living* LP produced by Island records which Burning Spear released in Jamaica retitled *Marcus Children*.

"The Prophet" featuring the deejay Big Joe was released on a seven-inch and is a deejay version of "Throw Down Your Arms" that was released the previous year. The song was then licensed to the Tribesman label in the UK and was released on 12inch in 1979 misspelled "The Profit".

"Dry and Heavy" was released as 7inch single with the b side dub version named as "School Days"

From the *Marcus Children* album "Marcus Children Suffer" was renamed and released as 7inch entitled the "Whole A We Suffer" in 1978.

1979 saw the last single released on the "Spear" label, "Nyah Keith". The song is a renamed reworking of "Zion Higher" from the Studio One period, is taken from the "Marcus Children" album that was released the previous year.

The 1980s saw a decrease in the output of singles by Burning

Spear though he continued to release pressings of his albums produced by various label and launched the *Living Dub* series.

Dub albums having become quite popular, Burning Spear launched a series of albums featuring dub versions of some of his tracks. This series spanned five volumes simply entitled *Vol 1, Vol 2* etc…

One of Burning Spear's highly regarded albums *Hail H.I.M* was released that year by EMI and in Jamaica it was available on the Burning Spear label.

"Bad To Worse" was released as a seven-inch single in 1980 an this version does not appear on a studio album although it was later included in a deluxe edition of the *Marcus Children* album, which leads us to believe that it was recorded at the time of that album and perhaps was cut from the track-list of that album. The song was rerecorded in 1983 for the *Fittest of the Fittest* album and the name slightly altered to "Bad To Worst"

That same year Burning Spear released a twelve-inch pressing of "Jah No Dead/Free The Whole Wide World" which was also released under license by the Tribesman label for the British market.

1981 saw the release of just one single, "African Teacher" taken from the *Hail H.I.M* album and pressed as a 45 on the Burning Spear label. Interestingly the song would be released in France by Panach, a company owned by Heineken, as a promotional single. The release paired the song "African Teacher" with Jimmy Cliff's "Oh Jamaica" on a seven-inch single and was licensed by the EMI label who had released the *Hail H.I.M* album. The single was not destined for sale but released as part of giveaway series of four records of different styles of music organised by the Panach company.

In 1982 "Education" was released as a seven-inch single on the Burning Spear label and also saw a new imprint called Marcus Music feature songs from other artist on three seven-inch singles.

"Education" was taken from the *Farover* album, released by Heartbeat, and pressed in Jamaica by Burning Spear's label while the same year he also released Vol 2 of the *Living Dub* series.

The Jomos sing their second and last release ("Old Time Religion") while singer Anthony Bradshaw and the group The Shambas see their only know release appear on separate seven-inch singles.

1983 saw the release of only one seven-inch single on the Burning Spear label entitled "Repatriation". The single was taken from the album *The Fittest of The Fittest* which was released the same year by the American label Heartbeat.

There were no studio albums released in 1984, but the Marcus Music label was revived for its last known production. The song "Jah Nuh Dead", which bears no relation to the Burning Spear song of the same name, featured DJ Niger Ranking on a seven-inch single. Interestingly though the deejay clearly pronounces his name as "Nigger", it is, perhaps intentionally misspelled "Niger" on the record label. It is the only known song by this artist.

The next album to be was released was *Resistance* in 1985, which was released by Heartbeat, with Burning Spear's label pressing copies for the Jamaican market. The single "A The Force" was taken from that album and pressed the following year in 1986. That year also saw the release of "Little Love Song" on a 45 taken from the album *People Of The World* released on the Slash label (owned by Warner Music) and with copies pressed in Jamaica by Burning Spear's label.

Though there were no studio albums released in 1987 the very nice "Mandela Marcus" was released as a seven-inch record. This song does not appear on any studio album, but does sound as if it was recorded during the sessions for the *People of The World* album. The song draws a comparison between Marcus Garvey and Nelson Mandela, who at the time of release was still a prisoner of the South African Apartheid regime. Burning Spear joined the cohort of Jamaican artists calling for his release, while reminding the listener that Marcus Garvey was an ardent defender of the rights of all Africans to self-determination and freedom.

From 1988 up to 1991 there were no single releases at all and the only output by the Burning Spear label was the Jamaican pressings of the *Mistress Music* and *Living Dub Vol 2* LPs in 1988.

In 1990 Burning Spear set up a new imprint for his productions named Rasta Business and released the Jamaican pressing of the *Jah Kingdom* album, originally released on Island Records' subsidiary Mango.

In 1991 the Burning Spear label featured "Come Come" as its only seven-inch single for the year. The song does not appear on any studio album and encourages the listener to be resolute in taking on the tasks that are necessary for a better world, with the help of Jah.

1992 saw a return to the use of the short-lived Rasta Business label which only put out six releases in total, four featuring Burning Spear material, and two featuring songs by Imani and D. Collar. Two Burning Spear singles were released in 1992, "Don't Sell Out" and "Burning Reggae", both on 45. "Don't Sell Out" would later appear on the *Appointment With His Majesty* album, released by Heartbeat in 1997, while "Burning Reggae" does not appear on any studio album. The song is a tribute to the reggae genre, and a sort of promotional piece endorsing the greatness of Jamaica's most influential musical offering to the world.

The next release for the label ("Mi Gi Dem") came in 1993 as a seven-inch single taken from the album *The World Should Know*, which came out the same year. For this release, Burning Spear reverted to the use of his Burning Spear label and as always, Jamaican pressings of the album were released.

In 1995 the Rasta Business label put out two singles by new artists Imani and D. Collar. Imani is featured presenting a song entitled "Nah Jester" and he has since released two other singles on other labels. These two seven-inch singles would appear to be the final releases on the Rasta Business imprint and more generally by any of Burning Spear's labels. Vinyl sales having plummeted in the 1990s, one can assume that Burning Spear decided they were no longer viable forms of release. 1995 also saw the release of the *Rasta Business* album on Heartbeat with Jamaican pressings being issued by the Burning Music label.

The following album, *Appointment With His Majesty*, was released on CD only in 1997. Interestingly the same year *Living Dub Vol3* was released by Heartbeat and it seems that it was not pressed at all by the Burning Spear label. In 1999, Heartbeat produced the successful *Calling Rastafari* album and the Burning Spear label returned to pressing the Jamaican copies.

In 2002, *Live in Montreux*, a live album was released by the French label Nocturne and Burning Spear released copies destined for the American market. The collaboration with Nocturne continued in 2003 with both CDs and vinyl being pressed by the Burning Spear label for the American market and in 2005 with the album *Our Music*. The last known album, *Jah Is Real* was produced and released by the Burning Spear label alone and appears to be the only instance of an album entirely produced and released without collaborating with an international label.

There are five vinyl releases that we were unable to date or to positively associate with Burning Spear.

Firstly "Jamaican DJ" by Daddy Bush is quite an unusual release because, as the label states, it was produced by one "M Miller" and the recut of the Bangarang riddim it features was produced by Bobby O'Hare for his X Rated label. It would seem to be the only instance where Burning Spear released music by an artist using a riddim not produced by himself or the label he was collaborating with. There are various songs on this riddim that were released by O'Hare and one can speculate that perhaps he decided not to release Daddy Bush's tune and for some reason Burning Spear agreed to release it on his own imprint. All other songs released on this version of the riddim came out in 1995 so it is likely that this record was released in 1995 or 1996.

There is a blank label seven-inch of "Jah See and Know" from the *Hail H.I.M* album that is said to exist but it seems hard to believe this is a legitimate Burning Spear release. The main reason being that no labeled pressing ever came out and although blank label pre releases are far from uncommon in the Jamaican recording industry there are no known instances of Burning Spear's label ever releasing any. It seems reasonable to suggest that this is a pirate pressing.

Similarly in the early 2000s, two seven-inch releases appeared on the market. Though they have the normal deep blue Burning Spear label on the records, the printing is of poor quality.

Furthermore and unusually these release have different vocal tracks on sides A and B with songs taken from different albums. One of them features "Hail H.I.M" on side A and "Dry And Heavy" on side B, while the other features "Man In The Hills" on side A and "Foggy Road" renamed "Road Foggy" on side B`. The audio quality is very poor on these releases and all these various incongruities suggest that these two releases are in fact pirate pressings that have nothing to do with the Burning Spear company.

When one looks over the span of Burning Spear's career it becomes clear that quite early on he had a desire for at least some independence in terms of creativity and the more down to earth matter of the business side of being an artist. Relatively early on in his career he decided to start a label that would have various imprints over the years and would release material destined to the market if the country where he was living. Though he was nearly always collaborating with big labels that would produced the albums, he made sure to include the right to press copies for his home country market as well as to be able to press singles that were often taken from albums but also songs that were standout singles.

Of the thirty-three singles released by his label, most tended to feature Burning Spear himself, but occasionally he would feature other artists. Interestingly , all of the artists that appeared on his label were completely unknown and most of them did not record anymore for Burning Spear or anyone else.

One of Spear's main influences is Marcus Garvey who was a staunch advocate of self-reliance, independence and black capitalism. Burning Spear's label is a testament to the fact that he does not simply agree with and spread Garvey's message, but has put it into action in his own business affairs. If any proof is needed that he has done so in an objectively successful way, one can look at the resale value of some of Burning Spear's releases which have become collector's items that are bought and sold at prices that can reach triple digits. All in all, the Spear, Burning Spear, Marcus Music and Rasta Business imprints have spanned over nearly fifty years and remain somer of the most successful labels run by an artist himself in Jamaican music and have provided music lovers and particularly vinyl collectors with some of the best that singles and albums that reggae has to offer.

56

IV
Is The Spear Still Burning?
(Moqapi Selassie)

On Monday 22nd July 2002, it was my pleasure and honour to share the stage with two giants of Reggae music – the legendary Burning Spear and Johnny Clarke. Honestly, it does not seem so long ago. Twenty-one years? Really? Nah man, the poster must be wrong! The show was held at the Hummingbird, Dale End, Birmingham, where, coincidently, I had made my dub poetry "debut" way back in the 1980s.

Even that debut could be seen as an epiphany, something that was not meant to happen - but it did. At the time, I was a member of the Birmingham Local of the Ethiopian World Federation Incorporated, which had about 150 to 200 mainly Rastafari members. A group of InI used to get together, with acoustic guitars, nyabinghi drums and other percussion instruments and jam, chant, make up songs, and have a good time. Then, as time passed, InI got electric guitars and a drum kit and we were in the process of taking it to the next level when we were told that we had a show at the Hummingbird in a week's time, or "a strong's time" as the Rastas would say (as "week" is reminiscent of "weak", the Rastas say "strong". Get it?).

Yuh what? No way! InI had half a drum kit, a rhythm guitar, a bass guitar and two hand drummers. InI were not ready to do a show anywhere, never mind the Hummingbird. Yuh mad? Big, big Hummingbird? InI were asked what had InI been doing all this time and that, like it, or like it not, InI had to perform. So, InI decided to put some basslines to my poems, use the nyahbinghi drums and go and do the show. And that is what InI did. The reception was good. Incidentally, the next week InI performed at London University, at the School of African and Oriental Studies, and once again the reception was good. So that's how I started doing dub poetry. By 'accident.' Oh, by the way, Macka B, the "lyrics machine", was on my debut Hummingbird show all those years ago. Big up Macka B!!!

So, I'd been "doing" dub poetry since 1984 when I did that first stage performance at the Hummingbird. I see it like this, just like being born to be a Rastafari, I was born to be a dub poet. Called, sent, chosen…whatever. Put another way, dub poets, like Rastafari, are born, not made. InI are born not made and if InI are "lucky", InI get paid.

From what I can remember of that Burning Spear concert at the Hummingbird, there was a buzz at the time as it was one day before the 110th Anniversary of the birth of Haile Selassie I, on July 23rd. Selassie's birthday is a major Rastafari celebration. And also, as the poster proclaimed, *"This tour is rumoured to be Burning Spear's last UK tour. This may be your last chance to see the Legend."* Whether that was true or not, it was an excellent marketing ploy, as on that night the Hummingbird was "ram-jam super jam", as the Jamaican saying goes.

Rastafari and reggae music lovers from all over the UK and Europe were in attendance. Yes, it was to see Burning Spear, but some came to see Johnny Clarke, another legend, and, if that wasn't enough, on the "wheels of steel", on his one record deck, playing his own sound system was none other than the legendary Jah Shaka. (who unfortunately is no longer 'trodding earth' today). This triumvirate of legends, this trinity of musical talent was just too good to be missed.

Representing Birmingham on the first show there was the 'Voice of Ujimaa;' a vocal outfit, and I, the Ras from Small Heath, Birmingham, the Ras people used to mock and ridicule when I said "I'm a dub poet". Not much has changed over the years except now people look with incredulity and ask, "what's one of them?" I then say I do "spoken word" and they nod and say "Oh" and walk off. By the way on the poster the promoters spelt my name wrong (*Maquapi Salassie*) but that's par for the course. C'est la vie.

Of the show itself, much of it remains a blur. From my perspective, it was the culmination of years of doing small "gigs" at community centres and schools, of doing carnivals and local festivals. I turned up, reported backstage, "hailed up" Johnny

Clarke, hung around front stage with my wife for a bit, then, I went backstage hailed up Burning Spear, went and did my performance in front of the biggest audience I had performed in front of at that time, delivered, got a great reception from I home town crowd and that was it. I had no reasoning with any of the two headline artists. InI had no bonding moments, or anything like that. No introduction, just a quick "Hail Rasta" in the corridor backstage as InI passed each other. That was it.

Looking back on that show now, it shows the mystical experiences InI have in life. Maybe life is a series of coincidences, a series of synchronicities connected by the mundane and the routine. Anyway, way back in the 1970s, I used to buy records. In those days, buying records was the fad, and it was the thing to do. Not only for lovers of reggae music but for all genres of music - pop music, soul music, classical music, jazz music, blues, rock and roll. Back in the day, people bought music.

In the Black community, almost every Black youth was into music. Pop, Soul, Reggae. Or, whatever music genre tickled his or her fancy. InI were into reggae music and sound systems, those large "mobile discos" that were all the rage back then. When I say that some were into sound systems you were either *in* a sound or *followed* a sound. Being in a sound meant that a group of people got together and built a sound system. They would buy music, obviously, build boxes with speakers, buy bespoke amplifiers and pre-amps, then play out and build a following. Really and truly, a sound system was a grassroots, ghetto enterprise. However, only a very few saw it as such. Back then, ones did it for the love of it.

Dances were kept at local community centres and church halls, or, when artists came from Jamaica, the clubs - which InI couldn't get into on a regular club night. These clubs were hired out to the reggae dance promoters, usually, on a Bank Holiday when the clubs were not being used by the usual patrons. These were big shows. Many artists passed through. The Wailers (the Original Wailers with Bunny and Peter), then later Bob Marley and the Wailers, Peter Tosh, Bunny Wailer, Dennis Brown, John Holt, Ken Boothe, Roy Shirley, The Mighty Diamonds, The Heptones, The Tamlins, Owen Grey, the Gaylads, Delroy Wilson, Desmond

Dekker, Dennis Al Capone, Big Youth, U Roy, I Roy, Fred Locks, the list goes on and on. It's endless. You name them, they came to Birmingham.

In those days, "blues dances" were the lick. They were kept in houses and the purpose was to have somewhere to go, to socialise, to hear *our* music and, of course, to make money. Drinks and food would be sold and later on, as years went by, an entrance fee would be charged.

I would buy records. With my cousin, who was/is an avid collector of reggae music, we would go to one of the local record shops along the Coventry Road in Small Heath Birmingham, Abi Records. This was just one of the stops in what became our Saturday afternoon ritual of touring the record shops in Small Heath (Aaron Records and Abi Records), Sparkbrook (Don Christie's), Handsworth (Tip Top, Zion Records), and The Bull Ring to get the latest, hip tunes, pre-releases hot off the press.

It was at Abi Records that I bought my first four reggae tunes. They were "Marcus Garvey" by Burning Spear; "Tribal War" by Little Roy", a no-name blank blue labelled instrumental tune featuring the melodica, I later learnt that it was by Bobby Kalphat, a contemporary of Augustus Pablo in that genre, all on pre-release: and, a released tune entitled "Move Out of Babylon" by Johnny Clarke. Those four tunes were like templates for I life. Those tunes that I bought on that Saturday afternoon were the start of a deeper journey for I. A journey into Rastafari, a journey into dub poetry, a journey into "getting to know I Self", to paraphrase the reggae icon Dennis Brown.

Burning Spear's "Marcus Garvey" raised questions in my mind. It got me thinking. Who was Marcus Garvey? "Marcus Garvey words come to paas Marcus Garvey words come to paas. Can't get no food to eat, can't get no money to spend!". Was he some sort of prophet? Wait deh, was there a Jamaican prophet? What did he prophesy? What did he do? When did he live? Was he like the prophets in the Bible? Who was Bagga Wire? How did he betray Garvey? What did Bagga Wire do? What were the words that Marcus Garvey said that had "come to pass"? What was he? That song just got my mind racing: questions, questions,

questions. I had to find out more about him. I had to find out about Black History, our story. I had to find out about Rastafari.

In school I was taught about 1066 and all that. I was taught about the Angles and the Saxons, the Norman Conquest, Magna Carta, Sir Walter Raleigh, *'Honi soit qui mal y pense'* ("Shame be to him who thinks ill of it"). I was taught about the sanitised history that was force-fed us in Denis Richards' *An illustrated History of Modern Britain 1789-1945*. I was taught all these things and more; but as Dennis Brown had sung "What about the half that's never been told"? It was this "half" that I needed to know. It was this that my generation needed to know. It was this half that Burning Spear's "Marcus Garvey" hinted at. And as a Rastafari elder once told me, "a hint is enough for a wise man". The search for "more knowledge" had begun.

I remember asking my mother about Marcus Garvey. She was a daughter of St Ann, Jamaica, the same parish that Marcus Garvey, and coincidentally Burning Spear, came from. So, I thought that she must know something about him. She did. She said he was a "troublemaker". And that was it. If that was so, I reasoned to myself back then, then why would all these reggae songs be made about him? I asked my brothers and sisters, those that were born in Jamaica, and they knew nothing about him. Something didn't add up. The quest continued.

The first book I got about Marcus Garvey was *Black Moses* by David Cronon. Looking back at it now, Cronon portrayed Marcus Garvey as an eccentric, a bit of a black Walter Mitty. A Black Jamaican man who went to America and had the curiously, grandiose notion of organising Black people internationally and returning some to Africa to build a strong Black nation. Surely, this was a madman. He just could not be right in the head. The book at least took Garvey out of the realm of myth and apocryphal hearsay and into the realm of palpable reality. Touchable.

He was not an ancient prophet clothed in burlap, or what Jamaicans called "crocus bag", but he functioned in the earlier part of the 20th century, the very same century that we were in back then. In fact, he died in London in 1940. He was my great grandfather's age, from that era. He had set up an organisation, a newspaper, factories, restaurants, and a shipping line. He was an orator, poet and newspaper editor. More importantly, by his actions he transformed the thinking of Black people globally. He inspired a paradigm shift for African people internationally. Marcus Garvey not only talked the talk, he also walked it.

One day at the Small Heath Community Centre, where the local Black unemployed youths used to gather, someone came with a book titled *Philosophy and Opinions,* by Marcus Garvey. Are you serious? A book? He had a philosophy? He had opinions? Reading from the book was revelatory. This was no buffoon, no clown or hustler. No, this was a man on a mission. He was the real deal. That book that I held in my hand that day proved that all InI had been taught was to mislead us, to brainwash us and that we didn't really know a quarter of what we should know. So yes, Burning Spear and the other Rastafari artists triggered a revolution, a revolution of consciousness. A paradigm shift. *A Rastafari revolution.*

Looking back, Johnny Clarke's "Move out of Babylon", which told the Rastaman to move out of Babylon and leave all the "wicked men" also left InI with a lot of questions to be answered. What is Rastafari? Where is Babylon? Who is Babylon? Who were these "wicked men"? How was the Rastaman going to move? And, more importantly, where to? "The Kingdom of Jah the Almighty?" Where was that? How was this move going to happen? And, when? As for 'anything you can do Rasta can do it better? What? Better? I'll have some of that. "Good, better, best never let it rest until your good is better and your better best". Surely, anything would be better than this. So, yes, you guessed it: the quest continued. Where were the answers to be found?

It was in the music, by word of mouth. Books and such came later. Even if they, the books, were out there, we could not get them there and then, as they were not accessible. There was no internet back then, there was no Google. In many respects the music, the sound systems, the reggae artists were *our Google.* That was our information highway. The music papers and magazines, such as *Black Echoes* and *Black Music* as well as the occasional article in *The New Musical Express* were the formal, mainstream media that kept the general public abreast of what was happening over in Jamaica and also in the UK, but it was the sound systems and the music that did it for InI. The sounds were immediate, straight away, "up-to-the-time". So, the music was the key. And to hear the music, InI went to dances.

Dances back then were more than just dances. They were moments to treasure. Dances were epiphanies. They were happenings. Yes, we went to socialise, to dance, to meet girls/young women, drink and smoke, but also to listen to the music. To hear what the sound systems were playing. How the sound played, and, if there was more than one sound, who played the best, who sounded the best, who rocked the people and edified them. The people were the judge and jury. On many occasions, one tune, one particular song, would "win" a dance. Many dances became memorable just because of a certain tune that was played in it. For example, I remember that dance when the Sufferer sound system from London played six dub cuts to Matumbi's "After tonight"? The people were not reactionary: they took part, they danced and they sang along to the tunes. Word for word, tune after tune.

What became known as "Roots Music" or "Roots and Culture Music" was our teaching tool. It was what "woke up" a generation. For the youths in England, roots and culture music was equivalent to a school, a college, a university. The artists, the singers and players of instruments were our teachers, our lecturers; the dances were our lessons, our seminars. Going to dances was the schoolroom. Rastafari, Black Consciousness, Racial and Social Uplift were the subjects. It was there that InI learnt about Marcus Garvey, Paul Bogle, Sam Sharpe, Haile Selassie I, Nanny, Dreadlocks, Ital food, Babylon, Class struggle, Africa being Zion, Babylon being the downpressor, Black Pride, Self-Development, Nyahbinghi, Peace and Love, Self-Reliance, Marijuana, Repatriation, Reparation, the list goes on. Dances were the engine rooms of what became known as the "golden age of Reggae music", the 'Rastafari revolution.

The singers and players of instruments were *the revolutionary vanguard*, and Burning Spear was one of the major players in that movement. It could be said that he was the initiator of the genre. Listen to his Studio One recordings, like his first tune, "Door Peep", from 1969 and then let me know. If his song "Marcus Garvey" sent tremors through the music industry, his first album for Island records of the same title sent shockwaves. The seminal, groundbreaking, epoch-defining *Marcus Garvey* is a roots and culture classic. Burning Spear won the Grammy, twice, for *Calling Rastafari* (1999), and *Jah is Real* (2008), but those albums cannot compete with *Marcus Garvey* in terms of impact. That album was seismic. It was like a tsunami. It heralded a new wave within reggae music. Roots and Culture had arrived. In terms of dramatic entrances, The Wailers' *Catch A Fire* prised open the door – Burning Spear's *Marcus Garvey* album kicked the door off its hinges.

Burning Spear and the other Rastafari artists triggered a revolution, *a revolution of consciousness*. A Rastafari revolution. One of the leading teachers at that time was Burning Spear. There was just something about his voice, its rawness, that, and the harmonies that just hooked you. Burning Spear differed from the sweet, mellifluous vocals of the Heptones, or The Mighty Diamonds or any other harmony group of the 1960s and 1970s. Those groups' vocals were smooth and honey-coated. They tickled your eardrums, enticing you to listen. Spear's vocals were rough and rugged. You had to listen - whether you wanted to or not. There was *roots* and then there was *deep roots. Burning Spear was deep roots.*

We can all agree that with regards to reggae music, Burning Spear is a musical giant. Also, for me, being on the Burning Spear show all those years ago was a fantastic experience.

However, there is something that has been troubling me recently, and it's about Rastafari in general, and the Rastafari singers and players of instruments in particular. It's about the role of that "Revolutionary Vanguard" as I have put it. It's about Covid 19, Repatriation, and Rastafari.

It was while reasoning (in Tanzania) with the elder Saburi Omega, a Rastafari elder who has been in Tanzania for 34 years that the "reasoning" turned to Repatriation and Rastafari. The reasoning was so poignant and pertinent because InI were at Almasi Street, Mbezi Beach, Dar es Salaam the "beachhead" for Repatriation in Tanzania. These two adjacent lands had been purchased by three Rastafari pioneers, Bupe Karudi, his wife Kisembo Karudi, and Professor Ken Edwards (aka Joshua Mhkululi) and were earmarked for Repatriation. These lands were to serve as a 'repatriation hub' and this was what it was initially used for. However, Professor Mhkululi and Ras Bupe both passed away and the Professor's 'portion,' was sold by his wife which was disputed by the Rastafari on the land and it ended up in a court case. Subsequently the Rastafari lost the case and the land became divided. Whither now Repatriation?

Anyway, it was during this reasoning that the role of the Rastafari singers and players of instruments and their role as a revolutionary vanguard came into question. After all, one of the many Rastafari mantras goes like this: "Repatriation is a must!" Where then were the Rastafari? Where were the singers and players of instruments? How comes the Rastafari singers that had promoted Repatriation in their songs had never made the journey to Africa and stayed? How comes they hadn't relocated? Where were they? Why hadn't these singers and players of instruments that had spread the message of Rastafari globally made that final journey to live in Africa? Where were the singers who had declared their undying love for Africa? Yes, where are they? Where was the action that needed to be taken by Rastafari, in general, and the Rastafari singers and players of instruments in particular?

Why after they had left the island paradise of Jamaica admittedly with all its woes, they invariably ended up in America or Europe but not on the African continent? Not Ethiopia, not Ghana, Kenya, Tanzania, The Gambia, South Africa, or wherever? Why America? Why the UK? Surely, the bright city lights of Babylon were/are not more alluring than the "paradise" of Africa? Questions, questions, questions.

One of the singers that came up in the reasoning is Burning Spear. Basically, the reasoning goes, after singing some of the most influential songs in reggae music, centred around Marcus Garvey and his teachings, Africa, African uplift and redemption, self-reliance, self-determination, and repatriation, amongst a host of other topics, why is Burning Spear living in New York? Why isn't he practising what he preaches, why isn't he living in Africa? Why isn't he walking the talk? To put it plain and straight: "Is the Spear still burning?" I hope people do not think I am singling out the Spear; that I am picking on him. I'm not. The same applies to many Rastafari singers and players of instruments; and Rastafari in general. The same applies to myself.

You see, within Africa/Black Culture, the singers and players of instruments have been looked up to by the general public. Many are revered; their music and they themselves have been held in high esteem. This is why I have called them the vanguard. If, however, the vanguard having sung of Africa as paradise, as Zion, but do not go there, to I man it's not good. It makes what they have been professing all these years appear like a 'fleeting illusion to be pursued but never attained.'

During the height of the pandemic when the so-called authorities were using all means of propaganda to persuade the general public to take the various vaccinations, Burning Spear came on the social media singing that people should be 'patient and take the vaccine. What would possess him to do such a thing?

The man who had retired, the man who hadn't sung a song in earnest for a number of years, the man who had stopped touring, was telling his fans and anyone who would listen to queue up, to comply and do what Babylon told them to do when his whole career was built on questioning and highlighting the duplicity of Babylon. It just didn't make sense. And it is this that has lead I to ask the question: 'Is the spear still burning?'

Was it because Babylon had threatened that if artists didn't take the vaccine they wouldn't be able to tour and the prospect of not being able to do that spurred Burning Spear to do what he did? Or, was it out of a genuine concern that people were dying and that at the height of the pandemic taking the jab was, he thought, the best thing to do? I do not know and I suppose only he can say.

Perhaps the question "Is the Spear still burning?" could be asked about the whole Rastafari movement. It could be asked about repatriation and the concept of African liberation and uplift. Are there still Rastafari out there that are still passionate about these ideals? Or, does it mean that "Resistance is Futile", and that the fire which once burnt bright over time fades away ? Who knows ? As Bob Marley once sang, "Time will tell".

V
Burning Spear's Legacy
and Influence
(Eric Doumerc)

Winston Rodney's contribution to Jamaican music and Jamaican culture cannot be overestimated and his status has been that of Reggae's elder statesman for many years now. His first album on Island, *Marcus Garvey*, started a whole new trend in reggae music and definitely put Marcus Garvey on the map. The figure of Marcus Garvey became a favourite topic with many young and aspiring reggae singers and bands in the 1970s.

 In 1975 Fred Locks had a very big hit with "Black Star Liners", a song that reminded Jamaican people of the legend about Garvey's ships coming into Kingston harbour to repatriate black people to Africa.

The Mighty Diamonds, a 1970s roots harmony trio, referred to Garvey in quite a few songs like "The Right Time", their first hit, but also on "Them Never Remember Poor Marcus". All these songs inscribed Marcus Garvey into the already well established oral tradition and extended that tradition with fresh input. So Spear's influence built upon the Jamaican oral tradition and extended it through reggae.

The reggae harmony trio Culture's first hit, "Two Sevens Clash", is supposed to have been based on a prophecy made by Marcus Garvey, even though Jospeh Hill repeatedly came up with new interpretations of that song. As indicated by Laura Tanna in her book entitled *Jamaican Folk Tales and Oral Histories*, Marcus Garvey's prophecies are part of the Rastafarian oral tradition (Tanna 54-56) and have been circulating for a long time in Jamaica. In June 1973, Tanna recorded a story related by one of her informers, known simply as Bongo, which is similar to the one told by Hill in "Two Sevens Clash": "He prophesy again dat witin dat said time, Kingston and Spanish Town shall meet" (Tanna 55-56). Barry Chevannes also mentioned the same prophecy (redemption will come when Kingston meets St Catherine) in his study of the Rastafarian movement (Chevannes 106).

Another prophecy mentioned in "Two Sevens Clash" and other reggae songs concerns the fact that Marcus Garvey was imprisoned in Spanish Town prison and that when he was released he predicted that no one would ever use the prison's gate again: "De gate dat he came tru, he said dey would never carry anoda man of his category tru dat gate but it shall seal" (Tanna 55-56).

In "Two Sevens Clash", Joseph Hill also mentions a cotton tree which was struck by lightning outside Ferry police station. In fact there was a cotton tree outside the police station in Ferry. It was known as "Tom Cringle's cotton tree" and was struck by lightning on 18 January 1971 (Senior 489), which blocked the nearby road for some time. Hill seems to have transferred this event to the year 1977 to create a dramatic effect. It must also be said that the cotton tree, also known as the silk cotton tree, is an important tree in Jamaican culture as it was beneath a cotton tree that obeahmen would bury the shadow of a living person in order to harm that person. If that shadow was not restored, the person could die. So the cotton tree is associated with witchcraft (or obeah), magical powers, non-Christian beliefs, and the fact that it was struck by thunder and lightning may suggest God's disapproval of the way colonial authorities treated Garvey.

The impact of the song was quite spectacular, and in *Catch a Fire*, Timothy White wrote that "On July 7, 1977, the Defence Force was on maximum alert in Jamaica and the streets were deserted. Despite official government bulletins that all was well, the majority of the citizenry declined to leave their homes, so potent had been the suggestive power of Culture's record."

According to White, the song was actually a prophecy based on the Book of Revelation in which St John the Divine had predicted the Apocalypse. The Book of Revelation contains many references to the number "seven"(the seven lamps of fire, the seven spirits of God, the book with the seven seals, the seven angels) which is associated with magical potency.

Thus the song is based on the resort to potent Jamaican symbols which are extremely suggestive and could be variously interpreted. Nevertheless, White's insistence that there is a strong apocalyptic and biblical element in that song seems to be borne out by the general tone of the song and by the use of the verb "to prophesy".

The *Marcus Garvey* album was one of the most listened to LP in the 1970s and several songs on the album were covered by other reggae artists, like "Slavery Days" which was rerecorded by Third World on their first album, and "The Invasion" which was recut by Jackie Edwards. Third World had also incorporated "Slavery Days" into their live set before recording their first album. Joe Higgs recorded a kind of sequel to "Slavery Days", entitled "More Slavery" with the same horn riff. Other reggae acts from the 1970s, like Junior Ross and the Spears and Reggae George were influenced by Burning Spear.

Jack Ruby produced other artists who recorded in the same mode as Spear, like The Skulls who had a minor hit with a track entitled "Black Slavery Days" (aka "Bondage") which was characterised by the use of horns and a similar theme. An album was released on the Clappers label with the same title and featured other artists working in the same Spear-influenced mode. Ruby also produced other harmony trios like Foundation and Link and Chain who owed something to Spear's music.

In 1970s Britain young black people were looking to reggae as a source of inspiration and education, and, according to David Hinds, lead singer with Steel Pulse, Burning Spear can be credited with kickstarting Rastafarianism in England: "BurningSpear was like an outlet and a vehicle. He used his philosophy through the reggae music where we learned of Marcus Garvey. It was an era where blacks, especially blacks in England, wanted something to hold on to as far as a culture, because it was shown to us, time and time again, that we weren't a part of the British society. So when Burning Spear came with that, it was like a godsend. I would say Burning Spear was responsible for the birth of Rastafari in England" (Carter Van Pelt, 1995). The growth of a whole new brand of English reggae bands like Aswad, Steel

Pulse, Matumbi, Black Slate, and Black Roots was undoubtedly made possible by the availability of Spear's records at the time. Moreover Spear was backed by Aswad on his first London gigs in 1977, and this contributed to the legitimacy of Black British reggae at the time.

As Moqapi Selassi explains in his article, Burning Spear was a source of inspiration, a teacher and a mentor for many young people of Caribbean extraction in 1970s Britain, and his role in educating a whole generation of Black British and Jamaican people about the importance of Marcus Garvey cannot be overestimated.

Burning Spear's impact and influence have extended far beyond the world of reggae music and have reached other spheres. Indeed Spear's conscious approach has been a major force in the development of a poetic tradition in the Caribbean and his music has inspired numerous poets. The Miami-based Jamaican poet Geoffrey Philp considers Burning Spear a major influence on his art: "Burning Spear's music has been a major source of inspiration for me as a writer, particularly in my work exploring themes of black identity, cultural heritage, and social justice. Burning Spear's powerful lyrics and socially conscious messages have always resonated with me, and his music has been an important touchstone in my own artistic development.

In my novel *Garvey's Ghost* for example, I drew on many of the same themes and ideas that are present in Burning Spear's music, exploring the legacy of Marcus Garvey and the ongoing struggle for black liberation and empowerment. Similarly, in my poetry and other writings, I have often looked to Burning Spear's music as a source of inspiration, drawing on his powerful imagery and evocative language to explore a range of themes and ideas.

Overall, I believe that Burning Spear's music represents a powerful example of the ways in which art can serve as a force for positive social change. His music continues to inspire me and countless other writers and artists around the world, and his legacy as one of the greatest voices in reggae music is secure."

Philp sees Spear a an important reggae ambassador in America: "Burning Spear's music has become more firmly established in the USA since 1979. In that year, he won his first Grammy Award for his album "Jah Kingdom," which helped to introduce his music to a wider American audience. Over the years, Burning Spear has continued to tour extensively in the US and has built a large and dedicated fan base in the country.

Burning Spear's music has also been embraced by other artists and musicians in the US, particularly in the reggae and world music scenes. Many American musicians have cited Burning Spear as a major influence on their own work, and his music has been sampled and covered by artists from a wide range of genres.

In addition, Burning Spear's socially conscious messages of black empowerment and resistance have continued to resonate with American audiences, particularly in the wake of the Black Lives Matter movement and other contemporary struggles for racial justice. As such, his music has become an important touchstone for many Americans seeking to explore and engage with these issues."

Spear's influence in the world of Caribbean poetry was already visible in the late 1990s when an important book by the poet and critic Kwame Dawes was published: *Natural Mystic: Towards a New Reggae Aesthetic*. In that book, Dawes claimed that a new, reggae-based aesthetics was there, ready to be used to reinvigorate Caribbean poetry and he identified Burning Spear's approach as an important model to draw inspiration from. That model was associated in Dawes' book with the voice of the prophet. Thus Dawes identified Winston Rodney as an important reference point, together with Bob Marley and Lee Perry, in the development of a new Caribbean aesthetics.

In the United States, the New Orleans musician Ben E. Hunter identified Spear as a key inspiration. Spear came to New Orleans in the early 1990s and performed in a local club: "What really did it for me was Burning Spear. He came to this club called Jimmy's, uptown, and just his whole approach, you know, he was so tense. He had sweat pants on, and he had this raincoat which was almost like torn, like he just came off the street, and he gave such a powerful performance." Ben E. Hunter became well-known as a performing artist on the New Orleans reggae and folk/acoustic scene. He recorded several albums as a solo artist and with the local group The Crucial Roots Band, and that is all due to Burning Spear's influence: "Seeing his performance inspired me to get into reggae music. Before that, I had no formal training or any family members in music."

The Miami-based dub poet Malachi D. Smith remembers the impact Spear's music had in the 1970s in Jamaica: "I became aware of Burning Spear's music in the early 1970s. This was a unique period in Jamaica. In 1972, Jamaicans elected the Michael Manley government to power. It was widely said that Marcus Mosiah Garvey had prophesized that Norman Manley was 10 years late and Michael would be the leader of the country one day. This happened in 1972, while the brutal system of apartheid was meting out atrocities to Africans in South and Southern Africa. Radio disc jockeys like Errol Thompson, ET, began the trend of playing Burning Spear as his music spoke about the realities in South Africa and also at home. The Rastafarian movement also enjoyed or began to enjoy a certain amount of acceptance during this era, and so the music of Burning Spear spoke and became a soundtrack of Rasta and the realities of the Jamaican sufferer. Tunes like "Foggy Road", and "Old Marcus Garvey" became favourites In 1973, when Studio One released, *Studio One Presents Burning Spear*, Jamaicans' tastes were dominated by European and American influences, the acceptance of Rasta and roots music was shunned and frowned upon by the upper class and the status quo. But as the social and cultural revolution began to take shape, Manley marrying a black woman, Beverly Manley, who was reading news on prime-time Jamaican TV newscasts, police force, the Jamaican Constabulary Force (JCF) had its first native police Commissioner in the person of Basil Robinson, the army, the Jamaica Defence Force had its first native leader in Brigadier Rudolph Greene, which all made it easier for an artist like Burning Spear to achieve a following."

Burning Spear began to tour again in 2022 and released a "new" album (in fact recorded more than ten years before it was released), *No Destroyer*, in 2023. He is thus likely to spread his influence even more and will no doubt inspire many budding reggae artistes in the future. Maybe the most fitting conclusion to this brief evocation of Burning Spear's long career should come from one of his most fervent fans, an anonymous Jamaican radio listener who had this to say about the importance of Burning Spear on July 12th, 1991 on the New York programme "Midnight Ravers" on WBAI-FM: " I want to tell Burning Spear that is nuff nuff youths in the Caribbean apart from Jamaica that him had a big impact on. And sometimes I wonder if a man like Burning Spear really realize the impact that him really had. I remember when I was about 12 years old and Burning Spear in I-man head every day. And right now I-man educationally, intellectually speaking have reached certain heights due to Burning Spear. I-man know nuff man and man who couldn't read and write. Burning Spear give them hope. And I want the man fe continue, even when the man dead. Me want the man sing from him grave" (Van Pelt, 1998).

As this heartfelt tribute makes abundantly clear, the Spear has burnt for a very long time and will always keep burning.

Discography
(Roots Knotty Roots)

Singles

1970
Door Peeper *(Bamboo)*
Door Peeper *(Supreme)*
Free (Free Again) *(Bamboo)*
Free (Free Again) *(Studio One)*
Rocking Time *(Supreme)*
Walla Walla *(Banana)*
Walla Walla *(Supreme)*
1971
Zion Higher *(Banana)*
Zion Higher *(Supreme)*
1972
Creation Rebel *(Fab II)*
Joe Frazier *(Iron Side)*
New Civilization *(Iron Side)*
New Civilization *(Supreme)*
1973
Call On You *(Coxsone)*
1974
Ethiopians Live It Out *(Coxsone)*
Foggy Road *(Fab II)*
Foggy Road *(Coxsone)*
Get Ready *(Coxsone)*
Marcus Garvey *(Capo)*
Marcus Garvey *(Mart's)*
Marcus Garvey *(Fox)*
Swell Headed *(Coxsone)*
This Population *(Bongo Man)*
What A Happy Day *(Coxsone)*
1975
Creation Rebel *(Forward)*
Free Black People *(Spear)*

Give Me *(Fox)*
Man In The Hills *(Wolf)*
Resting Place *(Wolf)*
Travelling *(Clocktower)*
Travelling *(Spear)*
Zion Higher *(Coxsone)*
1976
Door Peep *(Island)*
Free Black People *(Total Sounds)*
Lion *(Island)*
Lion *(Wolf)*
Man In The Hills *(Island)*
Old Man Garvey *(Island)*
Slavery Days *(Mart's)*
Slavery Days *(Fox)*
Spear Burning *(Spear)*
Tradition *(Island)*
1977
Dry And Heavy *(Spear)*
School Days *(Spear)*
The Youth *(Spear)*
Throw Down Your Arms *(Spear)*
1978
Civilized Reggae *(Island)*
Come *(Island)*
Social Living*(Island)*
The Sun *(Burning Spear)*
The Whole A We Suffer *(Spear)*
The Youth *(Burning Spear)*
1979
Institution *(Spear)*
Natural *(Spear)*
Nyah Keith *(Spear)*
1980
Bad To Worse *(Burning Spear)*
Columbus *(Warrior)*
Free Black People *(Spear)*
Jah Jah No Dead *(Spear)*

1981
Education *(Radic)*
Education *(Burning Spear)*
She's Mine *(Radic)*
Columbus *(Jammin' Sound)*
Free Black People *(Tribesman)*
Jah Jah No Dead *(Tribesman)*
1982
African Teacher *(Burning Spear)*
African Teacher *(Panache)*
Far Over *(Radic)*
Jah Is My Driver *(Radic)*
1983
2000 Years *(EMI)*
The Fittest Of The Fittest *(EMI)*
Repatriation *(Burning Spear)*
1984
A The Force *(Spear)*
Door Peeper *(Coxsone)*
1986
Little Love Song *(Burning Spear)*
Happy Day *(Torso)*
People Of The World *(Torso)*
This Experience *(Torso)*
1987
2000 Years *(Island)*
Mandela Marcus *(Burning Spear)*
Old Marcus Garvey *(Island)*
Tradition *(Island)*
1988
Say You Are In Love *(Blue Moon)*
Tell The Children *(Blue Moon)*
1990
Civilization *(Mango)*
Great Men *(Mango)*
1991
Come Come *(Burning Spear)*
Estimated Prophet *(Arista)*

1992
Burning Reggae *(Rasta Business)*
Don't Sell Out *(Rasta Business)*
Here To Pick Up The Pieces*(Rasta Business)*
Warm And Sunny Jamaica *(Rasta Business)*
1993
Mi Gi Dem *(Spear)*
Mi Gi Dem *(Heartbeat)*
2000
As It Is *(Heartbeat)*

Albums

Studio One Presents Burning Spear, Studio One, 1972.
Rocking Time, Studio One, 1974.
Marcus Garvey, Fox/Island, 1975.
Man In The Hills, Island, 1976.
Dry And Heavy, Island, 1977.
Live, Island, 1977.
Marcus Children/Social Living, Island, 1978.
Living Dub, Burning Spear, 1979.
Hail H.I.M, EMI, 1980.
Farover, Heartbeat, 1982.
Living Dub Vol.2, Burning Spear, 1982.
The Fittest of The Fittest, EMI, 1983.
Resistance, Heartbeat, 1985.
People of The World, Slash, 1986.
Mistress Music, Slash, 1988.
Live in Paris : Zenith, Slash, 1988.
Mek We Dweet, Mango, 1990.
Jah Kingdom, Mango, 1991.
The World Should Know, Heartbeat, 1993.
Love and Peace : Live 1993, Heratbeat, 1994.
Rasta Business, Heartbeat, 1995.
Living Dub Vol.3, Declic, 1996.
Appoitment With His Majesty, Heratbeat, 1997.
Live In Concert 1997, Musidisc, 1998.
Living Dub Vol.4, Declic, 1999.
Calling Rastafari, Heartbeat, 1999.

Freeman, Nocturne, 2003.
Our Music, Burning, 2005.
Living Dub Vol.5, Collective, 2006.
Jah Is Real, Burning, 2008.
Living Dub Vol.6, Burning, 2008.
No Destroyer, Burning, 2023.

Compilations:

Harder Than The Rest, Island, 1979.
Reggae Greats: Burning Spear, 1985.
Chant Down Babylon – The Island Anthology, Island, 1996.
The Ulitmate Collection, Hip-O, 2001.
Behold The Spear Burning, Pressure Sounds, 2001.
Sounds from The Burning Spear, Soul Jazz, 2004.

Bibliography

Barrow, Steve and Peter Dalton. *Reggae- The Rough Guide.* London: Rough Guides, 1997.

Bradley, Lloyd. " 'The Time is Right': Reggae's Colossus Burning Spear on racism, rebellion, and returning to Britain", *The Guardian*, 8 August 2022.

Chevannes, Barry. *Rastafari – Roots and Ideology.* Syracuse University Press, 1994.

"Garvey Myths Among the Jamaican People", in Lewis and Bryan, eds, *Garvey: His Work and Impact.* Trenton, NJ: Africa World Press Inc., 1991[reprintedin 1994].

Clarke, Sebastian. *Jah Music.* London: Heinemann, 1980.

Davis, Stephen and Peter Simon. *Reggae Bloodlines: In Search of the Music and Culture of Jamaica*, Da Capo Press: New York, 1992 [first published in 1977].

Dawes, Kwame. *Natural Mysticism : Towards a New Reggae Aesthetic.* Leeds : Peepal Tree Press, 1999.

Forgie, Andell, "Burning Spear : Heading For The Top", *Jamaica Daily News*, 26 May 1975.

Gayle, Carl. "Marcus Garvey Meets The Rockers Uptown", *Black Music*, February 1976.

Goldman ,Vivien, "Error Inc", *Sounds.* 19 November 1977.

Henderson, Richard. "Review of *Social Living*". *The Beat*, Vol.14, #1, 1995.

Heselgrave, Doug. "Positive: An Interview With Burning Spear", *United Reggae*, April 2012

Howell, Peter."Jamaica Beckons and Sibbles is Listening."*Toronto Star* 26 April 1991

Jeffrey, Ranking and Don Snowdon, "Burning Spear", *Slash,* 1980.

Johnson, Linton, Kwesi. "Jamaican Rebel Music", *Race and Class*, Vol. xvii, N.4, 1976.

Joyce, Mike."Burning Spear: His Flame is True", *The Washington Post*, July 26, 1991

Katz, David. *Solid Foundation – An Oral History of Reggae.* London: Bloomsbury Publishing, 2003.

"A Beginner's Guide to Reggae Legend Burning Spear", *Fact*

Magazine.
"Fire In Babylon: Burning Spear", *Mojo*, September 2022.
Lewis, Rupert and Patrick Bryan. *Garvey: His Work and Impact*. Trenton, NJ: Africa World Press Inc., 1991[reprinted in 1994].
Masouri, John, "The Real Deal", *Echoes*, April 2009.
"Burning Spear: une vie de combats", *Reggae Vibes Magazine,* July-August-September 2022.
Paladino, Ed. "Burning Spear: The Power and The Glory". *The Beat*, April 1989.
Ryan, Alan. "Review of Mistress Music", *The Beat*, 1989.
Senior, Olive. *Encyclopedia of Jamaican Heritage*. Twin Guinep Press, 2003.
Tanna, Laura. *Jamaican Folk Tales and Oral Histories*. Kingston, Jamaica: Institute of Jamaica Publications Limited, 1984.
Thompson, Dave. *Reggae and Caribbean Music*. San Francisco: Backbeat Books, 2002.
Turner, Michael, "Sounds Almighty: 40 tunes in Tribute to Mr Dodd", *The Beat*, Vol.23, #6, 2004.
Van Pelt, Carter, "Roots ResurreXtion", *The Beat*, Vol.14 # 2, 1995.
Van Pelt, Carter. "Burning Spear: The Grateful Dread", *The Beat*, Vol. 17 #1, 1998.
Van Pelt, Carter. "All In The Family: This Business of Reggae", *The Beat*, Vol.23, # 2, 2004
Washburn, Jim, "A Reggae Mission for Burning Spear, Whose Tour Is Coming to Irvine". *The Los Angeles Time,* June 1 1990.

E-mail interviews with Ben E. Hunter, Chris Lane, Bernard "Touter Havey", Moqapi Selassie, and Malachi D. Smith.

Contributors

David Bousquet is a senior lecturer at the University of Burgundy in Dijon, France. He specialises in the study of Caribbean literature, poetry and popular culture with a particular emphasis on musical traditions and reggae. His research on song lyrics and performance poems focuses on the tension between orality and writing from the perspective of post-colonial and cultural studies.

James Danino is a reggae activist living in the south of France. He runs a blog called *Wisdom Knowledge and Understanding* as well as having written and created fanzines such as *I Leaf* and *Focus*. Additionally Sir James gives talks about the history of Jamaican music.

Eric Doumerc is a senior lecturer at the University of Toulouse-Jean Jaurès, in Toulouse, southwestern France. His research interests include Caribbean poetry, music, and the Caribbean oral tradition.

Moqapi Selassie is a dub poet of Jamaican parentage who was born in England and who has been writing and performing in the UK since the early 1980s. He was born and raised in Birmingham and thus belongs to the Black British generation, the children of Jamaican immigrants who settled down in the UK in the late 1940s and throughout the 1950s. His poems have been published in several anthologies and magazines. 2019 saw the relase of his CD entitled *Lyric Man* .

Michael Turner is the author of *Roots Knotty Roots, The Discography of Jamaican Music*, an ongoing research project which documents in detail over 100,000 singles.   He is   the former author of "Reggae Obsession" a column in *The Beat* devoted to the great Jamaican music of the past and its nearly forgotten artists. He has been playing "old hits" on the radio and in clubs for over thirty years. He is a retired doctor living in Northern California.